THE

ROAD HOME

a daily devotional guide

DAVID DEFFENBAUGH

little acorn
Growing tall oaks for God!

112 W. CALISTA DR.
TAHLEQUAH, OK 74464

Little Acorn, LLC
112 W Calista Dr
Tahlequah, OK 74464
www.littleacornkids.net

Printed in the United States
First Printing, November 2015

ISBN-13: 978-0-9964448-0-4

Dedication:

To my life's companion, Tanya, with gratitude and appreciation for your encouragement, support, strength, and mostly, your love.

Foreword

Regardless of what day today is, I will eat. If I haven't yet, I will. If I already have, I likely will again. Some food is necessary for life. Some is eaten not of necessity, but as a treat, some out of habit, and some for emotional reasons (think "comfort" food).

God's word is spiritual food. That food is eaten for precisely the same reasons as is physical food: nutrition, joy, habit, comfort.

No one has to tell me to eat today. No one has to encourage me. Exceedingly rare (if ever) have been the times someone had to remind me to take in food. My own appetites (physical and emotional) and habits are sufficiently honed so that no outside influence is really necessary. Psalm 119 reveals a person with a finely tuned desire for God's word. He's not reading because he has to, though he does have to. He's not reading because someone is pressuring him to do so, that pressure is internal and part of his nature. He's not reading out of obligation, absolute joy and delight flow from time spent in God's word.

It is my prayer that in some small way this book might serve to help further develop your appetite for the Bible; that somehow in you it will also be true that regardless of what day today is, you will consume God's word.

A debt of gratitude goes to Little Acorn—but really Tyrel and Justin Hatfield, the men behind the title—for its contribution to promoting daily reading of God's word by God's people through the publication of this (and other) books.

Gratitude is also extended to Ashley Deffenbaugh and Alison Eskew for sharing their skills and talents to provide proofreading and editing services for this book. Ladies, this book could not have happened without your help!

Finally, to the reader, may you learn more, love more, and be led more by God through His word.

God bless,
David Deffenbaugh

JANUARY

1

Daily Bible Reading: Genesis 1-2; Matthew 1

Where Did You Come From?

Devotional Text: Genesis 1:1

Both Genesis 1 and Matthew 1 tell about origins: where the created universe and all it contains came from, and where Jesus, physically speaking, came from. Where we come from is important. Isaiah said, "Listen to me, you who pursue righteousness, you who seek the Lord: look to the rock from which you were hewn, and to the quarry from which you were dug" (51:1).

Think about your origins. Think about your past, physically and spiritually. Think about your church family and all that has gone on before to bring it to the place it is today. Think about our culture and nation and all that has happened in days gone by to make it what we know today.

As you pray, thank God for all the good influences brought to bear on your life that have helped you be where and what you are today.

2

Daily Bible Reading: Genesis 3-4; Matthew 2

Ups and Downs

Devotional Text: Matthew 2:11

The child Jesus was an object of worship (by the wise men) and a murderous plot (by Herod). He came to call a despised town home (see John 1:46). Like Jesus' youth, life isn't always even-handed. It has its ups and downs. Life isn't defined exclusively by the good times, or the bad. As you identify both circumstances in your own life, how do you keep life from being a constant roller coaster of emotions?

3
Daily Bible Reading: Genesis 5-6; Matthew 3

My Sin

Devotional Text: Genesis 6:5

The effects of sin are devastating. It spoiled Paradise for Adam and Eve (Gen. 3), and it ruined Cain's life (Gen. 4). Now it threatens the whole of humanity (Gen. 6:5). What is the sin with which you now struggle? What can you do about it? What should you do? Improper handling will destroy. Not maybe. Not might. Not could. It will.

Think seriously about your sin. Pray to God. Do something about it. Now.

4
Daily Bible Reading: Genesis 7-9; Matthew 4

Overcoming Temptation and Satan

Devotional Text: Matthew 4:14

Satan tempted Jesus. Jesus emerged victorious.

Of course He did.

The means used by Jesus to overcome temptation was not a resource only available to God's own Son, creator of heaven and earth. He used the same means available to you and I. He met temptation with Scripture.

So, knowing the temptations with which you struggle, what Scriptures would help you be victorious? List them. Write them out. Learn them.

5

Daily Bible Reading: Genesis 10-11; Matthew 5:1-16

Distinctive or Indistinguishable?

Devotional Text: Matthew 5:13

"You are salt...you are light." At least that's what Jesus said. In other words, you are an influence in the world around you by virtue of following Jesus.

Really, though, is your concern more for blending in or for standing out? In what very real ways can you and should you, as a disciple of Jesus, stand out from the world?

6

Daily Bible Reading: Genesis 12-14; Matthew 5:17-48

Decisions Spiritually Made

Devotional Text: Genesis 13:10

Upon what did Lot base his decision when presented with a choice by his Uncle Abram (Gen. 13:10)? What price did he eventually pay for the decision made here? Think about what eventually happened to Lot and Sodom.

In the process of making the many decisions you face every day (some big, some very small), think about the spiritual implications of those choices. Are you willing to allow spiritual implications and influences to carry much weight as you make the choices that shape your life every day?

7

Daily Bible Reading: Psalms 1-4; Proverbs 1:1-19

My Greatest Delight

Devotional Text: Psalm 1:2

In what do you delight? Think about it. It could be just about anything. It's something that you enjoy, that is thrilling to you, and of which you just don't tire.

The "blessed" person is one whose delight is "the Law of the Lord" (Psa. 1:2).

Is it yours? If not, what steps can you take, starting today, to make it such?

8

Daily Bible Reading: Genesis 15-17; Matthew 6:1-18

Sinful Worship

Devotional Text: Matthew 6:1

Jesus warned about the practice of our acts of devotion. Seems strange doesn't it: sinning while we worship? The caution is about "practicing your righteousness...in order to be seen" by others.

So think about this. What if there was no church family? What if there was no group of like-minded people with which to assemble on Sundays and Wednesdays? Would you still worship? Would you still participate in study and times of devotion?

It's never comfortable and always difficult to honestly examine our motives, but it is necessary.

9

Daily Bible Reading: Genesis 18-19; Matthew 6:19-34

Impossible?

Devotional Text: Genesis 18:11

Why do we limit God? We may not mean to, but when we label--even if it's in our own minds--a situation or circumstance as impossible, we have done exactly that. Yet, surely one of the messages we must get from Scripture is that human limitations do not apply to God.

So, when it came to Abraham and Sarah having the child God had promised, it was highly improbable at the time of Abraham's call. He was 75 and Sarah 65 (see Gen. 12:4 & 17:17). By the time we get to Genesis 18, the Bible even says it: "Sarah was past childbearing" (v. 11; NASB). It was humanly impossible, but the fact remains: Isaac was born.

What is "impossible" in your life right now? For whom is it impossible?

"For nothing will be impossible with God" (Luke 1:37).

10
Daily Bible Reading: Genesis 20-21; Matthew 7

How Many?

Devotional Text: Matthew 7:13-14

We like options and lots of them. We tend to believe that people have lots of options spiritually. Is that because we want it to be that way or because God tells us it's that way?

We will do well to remember that Jesus said there are only two ways (Matt. 7:13-14). One leads to life, the other to destruction. We are on one or the other.

Those are our options.

11
Daily Bible Reading: Genesis 22-24; Matthew 8:1-22

Show Up!

Devotional Text: Genesis 22:1,7,11

It's said that 90% of being successful is just showing up. I don't know how you'd measure that exactly, but consider Abraham when God commanded him to offer his son Isaac (Gen. 22). Beyond the very obvious and impressive willingness to do what seems unthinkable as a parent, Abraham was called upon three times: by God (v. 1), by Isaac (v. 7), and by the angel (v. 11). Every time, Abraham responded the same: "Here am I."

He was there. He showed up.

Do we show up when we are called upon numerous times in our day by our spouses, our children, our parents, our bosses, our communities, our friends, our co-workers, our teachers, etc.?

JANUARY

12
Daily Bible Reading: Genesis 25-26; Matthew 8:23-9:13

The Hazards of Following

Devotional Text: Matthew 8:23

"...His disciples followed Him" (Matt. 8:23). Obvious isn't it? That's what disciples do; they follow.

This time they followed Jesus into a boat. That boat was headed across the Sea of Galilee and into the teeth of a life-threatening storm.

Following Jesus is not a guarantee of ease, safety, or comfort. Are we still willing to follow Him?

13
Daily Bible Reading: Genesis 27-28; Matthew 9:14-38

Am I Partial?

Devotional Text: Genesis 27

Partiality is a problem. James said we should never let it into the church (Jas. 1:1-13). Partiality fueled one of history's most notorious family feuds: Jacob and Esau's.

Partiality harms families, the church, friendships, and virtually any relationship.

Look closely. Be brutally honest. Am I guilty?

14

Daily Bible Reading: Psalms 5-8; Proverbs 1:20-33

Will God Hear Me?

Devotional Text: Proverbs 1:24-28

God does answer prayer. The Bible says so. But it also says that if we refuse to listen to God, He will refuse to listen to us (Prov. 1:24-28). Chew on that for a moment or two.

Prior to God hearing and responding to my prayers is my hearing and responding to God. Do I have the same fervor for the latter as I do the former?

Today, what is it that I know God would have me do that I have not done? Resolve to hear and respond to God so that He will hear and respond to you.

15

Daily Bible Reading: Genesis 29-30; Matthew 10

My Uniqueness in God's Service

Devotional Text: Matthew 10:2-4

"Jesus called them one by one; Peter, Andrew, James and John..." Did you ever learn that song? One lesson to be learned from Jesus' choice of the twelve apostles is that He wasn't interested in sameness. That is, this is a pretty diverse group of men. There were blue-collar workers (Peter, James, and John: the fishermen) and white-collar workers (Matthew: the tax collector). There were some very outgoing "upfront" kind of people (like Peter) and apparently some who just remained in the background (like maybe Bartholomew or Thaddaeus). There were also likely some wide-ranging political leanings. Matthew, as a tax collector, would have leaned more toward a pro-Roman stance, while Simon the Zealot would have been adamantly anti-Roman.

Jesus wasn't looking for people just like Himself. There wasn't a certain "type" He was going for. My own uniqueness is not a hindrance or deterrent from following Jesus. As long as I submit to His will, Jesus can use--and wants--all kinds.

16

Daily Bible Reading: Genesis 31; Matthew 11:1-24

Relationship Maintenance

Devotional Text: Genesis 31:2

One of the very most important features of our lives is our relationships. Some are good, some aren't. Some we choose, some choose us. Jacob's relationship with his father-in-law had been challenging from nearly the beginning. Remember it was Laban who switched brides on Jacob on his wedding night (see Gen. 29). Now, it takes another turn for the worse (Gen. 31:2).

Jacob decided it was time to end, or at least change, the dynamics of this relationship. He left Laban's house, took his wives (Laban's daughters), and went back home. It proved difficult to accomplish, but Jacob did leave, and it was definitely for the better.

What about the relationships of your own life? Are there any that need attention? Any that need to be ended, changed, or nurtured and revived?

17
Daily Bible Reading: Genesis 32-33; Matthew 11:25-12:21

Good Enough

Devotional Text: Matthew 11:28

Ever think you aren't "good enough" as a Christian? That you don't feel strong or you have more questions than answers or maybe even a sense of shame or guilt for past mistakes and failures?   Every one of us feels these or similar things more often than we'd like.

But here's the great news--that does not keep us from Jesus; far from it! He invites those who are "weary and carry heavy burdens" or "troubled and weighted down with care" (Matt. 11:28; NLT, BBE).

Weakness and burdens should never keep us from Jesus but be the very reason we come to Him.

18

Daily Bible Reading: Genesis 34-35; Matthew 12:22-50

Promises, Promises

Devotional Text: Genesis 35:11-12

Is there anything as fragile as a promise? They are so easily and frequently broken.

Not true with God. His promises are certain. Guaranteed.

His promise to Jacob (Gen. 35:11-12) is one of the most important in the Bible. It was a repeat of the one made to Abraham and Isaac. It's a promise that involves Jesus.

A promise is an assurance of what is not. God's promise is as sure as if it already is.

19

Daily Bible Reading: Genesis 36-37; Matthew 13:1-23

A Heart to Hear

Devotional Text: Matthew 13:15,19

Jesus was a master teacher. That doesn't mean everyone got what He was saying, though. As He explained His reason for using parables, Jesus said dull hearts prevent people from understanding (Matt. 13:15).

In the parable of the sower, Jesus said the seed that fell along the path and that the birds ate represents people who hear but don't understand God's word (13:19).

There's more to getting God's word than Jesus' unquestionable ability as a teacher. The condition of my own heart plays a major role. Pray that the Lord will help us to have open, sensitive, understanding hearts.

20

Daily Bible Reading: Genesis 38-39; Matthew 13:24-52

Made to Prosper

Devotional Text: Genesis 39:23

How would you like for this to be said of you? "The Lord was with him; and whatever he did, the Lord made to prosper" (Gen. 39:23). Wouldn't that be nice? Everything would be just like we wanted, right?

This statement is made about Joseph while he was in jail--after he acted righteously in refusing Potiphar's wife's seductions, after he'd been sold as a slave by his own jealous brothers, after he'd been hauled hundreds of miles away from his home and his father's house.

What do your circumstances have to be in order for you to think that God is with you?

21

Daily Bible Reading: Psalms 9-12; Proverbs 2:1-22

What Is God Up To?

Devotional Text: Psalm 10:1

Ever wonder what God was up to? Ever wonder why God wasn't doing what seems so clear to you that he ought to do? Ever feel like He wasn't listening, that He'd turned a deaf ear to your troubles?

You're not the first; and you're not alone.

"Why, O Lord, do you stand far away? Why do you hide yourself in times of trouble?" (Psalm 10:1)

In spite of what we may think or how we may feel, God is still God whether or not He's responding to us as we think He should.

22
Daily Bible Reading: Genesis 40-41; Matthew 13:53-14:36

Right Because It's Right

Devotional Text: Matthew 14:1-12

If you do the right thing, you expect things to go well, don't you? The only thing is, the Bible doesn't say that it's going to be that way all the time.

John the Baptist is certainly a case in point (Matt. 14:1-12). He did right. He stood for right. He died for it, too.

So, do I do right just so things will turn out well, or do I do right because it's right?

23

Daily Bible Reading: Genesis 42-43; Matthew 15:1-28

What's Going On?

Devotional Text: Genesis 42:1-2

As you read about Jacob's sending his sons to Egypt to buy grain, remember:

...it was due to a famine God had foretold to Pharaoh in a dream over 14 years earlier,

...the grain was available because God had empowered Joseph to interpret Pharaoh's dream and present a plan of action,

...it was bought from Joseph, whom God had raised from slave to prisoner to 2nd ruler,

...these same brothers had initiated this remarkable chain of events (orchestrated by God) by an act of jealous vengeance.

Next time we think we've got things all figured out--especially thinking we know what God should do, is doing, or has done--we better think again.

24

Daily Bible Reading: Genesis 44-45; Matthew 15:29-16:12

What Am I Going To Do?

Devotional Text: Matthew 15:34

When Jesus and the disciples discussed what to do about the problem of a hungry multitude, He asked them, "How many loaves do you have?" (Matt. 15:34).

What difference did that make? This was the one who walked on water, healed the crippled and sick, and raised the dead. This problem was a piece of cake, or bread as the case may be.

Jesus took the little bread they had and with it fed over 4,000.

We want to know what Jesus is going to do. He wants to know what we're going to do. So...what is that?

25

Daily Bible Reading: Genesis 46-47; Matthew 16:13-28

Influence For God

Devotional Text: Genesis 46:3-4

Joseph invited his father and all of his family to come to Egypt. God appeared to Jacob and told him not to be afraid to go (Gen 46:3-4). Jacob decided to go and the entire family, with all they possessed, went to Egypt.

God had intended for the descendants of Abraham to go there (see Gen. 15:13). But, it wasn't until Jacob made the decision that they went, and the family, in essence, then fulfilled the intentions and purposes of God.

We all have some sort of influence. There are people who watch the decisions we make, and their own decisions and actions are affected by ours.

Here's the question: based on what we do--or don't do--are people influenced in the direction of God's will?

26

Daily Bible Reading: Genesis 48-49; Matthew 17:1-23

Willing to Listen

Devotional Text: Matthew 17:5

The message of the transfiguration is found in the words spoken by God on the occasion: "This is my beloved Son, with whom I am well pleased; listen to Him" (Matt. 17:5).

Later in the New Testament we're told that God spoke at various times and in various ways in the past, "but in these last days has spoken to us by his Son" (Heb. 1:2). Add to that the warning, "See that you do not refuse him who is speaking" (Heb. 12:25).

When it's all said and done, the bottom line is whether or not we have actually listened to God through Jesus.

Well, have I?

27

Daily Bible Reading: Genesis 50; Exodus 1-2; Matthew 17:24-18:35

Cry Out

Devotional Text: Exodus 2:23-24

The people of Israel "cried out; and their cry for help because of their bondage rose up to God. So God heard their groaning; and God remembered..." (Ex. 2:23-24).

Did you catch all that? God's people were in bondage. They cried out to God for help. God heard them and remembered.

So, my bad circumstances do not mean God has abandoned or deserted me. In my hurting and pain I should cry out to Him. He will hear.

28

Daily Bible Reading: Psalms 13-17; Proverbs 3:1-12

Favor With God and Man

Devotional Text: Proverbs 3:3-4

Finding favor in the sight of God and man (Prov. 3:4) is a worthy achievement. Especially considering two other Bible personalities described in just those terms: Samuel (1 Sam. 2:26) and Jesus (Lk. 2:52).

How does one attain to such? "Do not let kindness and truth leave you; Bind them around your neck, Write them on the tablet of your heart" (Prov. 3:3).

With all that you have on your "To Do" list for the day, your goals for the month, your resolutions for the year, and the aspirations for your life, are kindness and truth even on your radar?

29

Daily Bible Reading: Exodus 3-4; Matthew 19:1-20:16

Attitude Toward Children

Devotional Text: Matthew 19:13-15

Some unidentified persons brought children to Jesus (Matt. 19:13-15). The desire was for Jesus to lay hands on them and pray.

The disciples did not respond well. Did they think Jesus too important to mess with mere children, His time too valuable to waste on insignificant ones, His time and energies better engaged in more profitable directions?

He, though, thought them quite important, well worth His time, and of great value. After all, the kingdom of heaven--that which Jesus came to initiate and to which I aspire--belongs to such as these.

Any attempt to match my priorities and values to those of Jesus must consider children.

30

Daily Bible Reading: Exodus 5-6; Matthew 20:17-21:11

Understand to Obey

Devotional Text: Exodus 5:2

"Who is the Lord that I should obey Him?" (Ex. 5:2).

Pharaoh's question was a good one. Who, indeed, is the Lord? Of course, he was about to find out. The impending plagues were the answer to that question. Only when duly impressed with God was he willing to allow Israel to leave Egypt.

My own willingness to obey God depends on my understanding of who God is. If I have an obedience problem, knowing God better is the answer.

31
Daily Bible Reading: Exodus 7-8; Matthew 21:12-32

Cleaning God's Temple

Devotional Text: Matthew 21:12-13

Turning over tables and chairs of money changers and dove sellers in the temple sufficiently demonstrated Jesus' displeasure (Matt. 21:12-13). Did it put an end to these nefarious activities? Likely not. No doubt, the tables were set upright, the coins collected, and order restored in short order.

What did Jesus' outburst accomplish? It shows His attitude toward the desecration of God's temple. God still has a temple. It is Christians, both individually (1 Cor. 6:19) and collectively as the church (1 Cor. 3:16).

Is God's purpose being fulfilled in God's temple today? Would Jesus do some house cleaning in me and in His church?

FEBRUARY

1

Daily Bible Reading: Exodus 9-10; Matthew 21:33-22:14

What Happens After Remorse?

Devotional Text: Exodus 9:27

Pharaoh said, "I have sinned" (Ex. 9:27). That's pretty remarkable. It would seem that he's come to an understanding. But has he?

Moses knew otherwise and said, "I know you do not yet fear the Lord God" (Ex. 9:30). Sure enough, as soon as this plague (hail) ceased, Pharaoh "sinned again and hardened his heart" (Ex. 9:34).

In our own spiritual quest, it is one thing to recognize our sin; it is quite another to fear God.

If you know you have sinned, that's good. That remorse, though, is not sufficient to prevent further failures. Only the genuine fear of the Lord can help guard us from sinful patterns of behavior.

2

Daily Bible Reading: Exodus 11-12; Matthew 22:15-16

When I Think I Have It Figured Out

Devotional Text: Matthew 22:29

Has anyone ever posed to you a hypothetical situation that in some way seemed to contradict or otherwise negate the Bible's teaching? I have heard many (it seems that most have had to do with the necessity of baptism).

When Jesus was confronted with such (this one aimed at the doctrine of the resurrection--Matt. 22:24-28), He said, "You are wrong because you know neither the Scriptures nor the power of God" (Matt. 22:29).

It really doesn't matter what we think we have figured out, what seems to make sense, or what we've decided doesn't make sense. Our mental energies are best devoted to knowing Scripture and the power of God.

3
Daily Bible Reading: Exodus 13-14; Matthew 23

What God Has Done

Devotional Text: Exodus 13:3

God wanted the people of Israel to remember concerning their deliverance from Egypt, that "by a strong hand the Lord brought you out from this place" (Exodus 13:3).

They did not remember. In later years, on several occasions, God's displeasure with them had to do with their attributing this incredible act of His compassion and deliverance to someone--or something--else. For instance, see Exodus 32:1-4. The consequence of such thinking was disastrous.

We dare not forget the good that God has done for us nor attribute His great works to anyone or anything else. The Bible begins by saying, "In the beginning, God created the heavens and the earth" (Gen. 1:1). However, today science says--or at least very vocal segments of it do--that a "big bang" is responsible for the heavens and the earth. Intellectual intimidation aside, such thinking is no less disastrous today.

4

Daily Bible Reading: Psalms 18; Proverbs 3:13-35

When Is The Problem

Devotional Text: Psalm 18:46

The 18th Psalm is ascribed to King David "when the Lord rescued him from...the hand of Saul." This praise of thanksgiving for God's deliverance is truly beautiful. Parts of it have been set to music and are sung even today: "The Lord liveth, and blessed be the rock and let the God of my salvation be exalted" (from verse 46).

Don't forget in all of this that David had spent several years in less than desirable circumstances running and hiding from the wicked and jealous King Saul. No doubt David would have liked these hard and stressful times to end sooner. Even so, he maintained his faith and trust in God.

Our most frequent complaint with God concerns His timing. He often doesn't do things when we'd like to have them done. Just because our deliverance has not happened yet does not mean it will not, or that God has forgotten us, or that He's not hearing us. David had his day of rejoicing, and so shall we.

5

Daily Bible Reading: Exodus 15-16; Matthew 24:1-35

Which Day?

Devotional Text: Matthew 24:34

Without doubt, Matthew 24 is a challenging section of Scripture. It helps to remember that Jesus speaks of two different days in this chapter. One day was to be anticipated and preceded with signs by which God's people would be able to know its approach and take appropriate action. This day would come in the lives of the generation then living and hearing Jesus (v. 34). This day refers to the destruction of Jerusalem by the Romans.

The other day, however, will be different in that "no one knows" when it will happen, "not even the angels of heaven, nor the Son, but the Father only" (v. 36). There will be no signs to signal its arrival. "Therefore you also must be ready, for the Son of Man is coming at an hour you do not expect" (v. 44).

Figuring out exactly what Jesus says will happen relative to each of these days can be challenging. What is not difficult is the point of all of this discussion for you and I now: Be ready!

Are you?

6

Daily Bible Reading: Exodus 17-19; Matthew 24:36-25:13

Not Alone

Devotional Text: Exodus 18:17-18

As Moses was leading the people of Israel out of Egypt and through the wilderness on the way to Mt. Sinai, they encountered Jethro, Moses' father-in-law. Jethro was duly impressed with all that God had accomplished through his former herdsman. However, with the workload Moses had taken on himself--judging the people from morning till evening--he was not impressed.

"What you are doing here is not good...you will certainly wear yourself out...You are not able to do it alone" (Ex. 18:17-18).

That's good advice. Are you trying to do too much? We may have an over inflated estimation of our own value and importance. "I have to do it." No, we don't have to do it all. Find others who can help. Empower someone else to take on tasks for which they are fully capable. Turn it loose. Let it go. Concentrate on those matters for which you are best equipped.

7

Daily Bible Reading: Exodus 20-21; Matthew 25:14-46

At Least One

Devotional Text: Matthew 25:14-30

Jesus' parable of the talents (Matt. 25:14-30) teaches numerous valuable lessons:

- We have all been bestowed with at least one talent from God.
- Not everyone has the same talents, nor the same number of talents.
- What we have is not our own, but God's who gave it. We are but stewards.
- Each of us has the responsibility to use what God has given to us.
- Fear is the enemy of the child of God.
- God's expectations of us are based on what He has given us (not what He has given someone else).

I know there are more than just these, but it's a start. So, what talents has God given to you (and don't limit your thinking to talents as abilities)? How are you using those to God's glory?

FEBRUARY

8
Daily Bible Reading: Exodus 22-23; Matthew 26:1-35

Two Commands

Devotional Text: Exodus 22:1-2

Reading through some of the specific commands of the Law of Moses in Exodus 22-23, one might wonder how the people of Israel kept up with all of these laws. There are so many, and this is just the beginning of so many more to come.

We would do well to remember that Jesus said that all of the Law is summed up in two commands: Love the Lord your God with all your heart and with all your soul and with all your mind; and love your neighbor as yourself (see Matt. 22:34-40).

If a person fulfilled these two, all the others would take care of themselves.

9

Daily Bible Reading: Exodus 24-25; Matthew 26:36-56

Do Not Forget to Pray

Devotional Text: Matthew 26:39

In Jesus' hour of crisis He prayed. The prayer(s) in Gethsemane is one of the most famous of prayers. Think about the circumstances. A mob is on the way to arrest Him. He knows death is imminent. The turn of events will bewilder and confuse His disciples. He's about to endure the unimaginable task of taking on Himself the sin of all humanity. His sorrow is crushing.

How does Jesus respond? He prays.

What are your worries and concerns and burdens and struggles? What challenges or people or tasks lie ahead of you?

Whatever else you may have already done or need to do to prepare for what lies ahead, no matter what, do not forget to pray.

10
Daily Bible Reading: Exodus 26-27; Matthew 26:57-75

God With Us

Devotional Text: Exodus 26:1

One of the tasks accomplished at Mt. Sinai after leaving Egypt was the construction of the tabernacle. This was going to be the place where God would meet His people. It contained the Holy Place and the Holy of Holies.

Think about this. The people of Israel were living in tents, moving through the wilderness. God was with them. He had His tent, His tabernacle. This was a visible representation of the fact that God was with them.

Some interesting terminology is used of Jesus when it says He "became flesh and dwelt among us" (John 1:14). Literally, it is saying He "tabernacled" among us. Remember one of the names for Jesus is Immanuel, "God with us" (Matt. 1:23). The Lord's presence with us is one of the key features of our relationship with Him. His promise is: "And behold, I am with you always" (Matt. 28:20).

11

Daily Bible Reading: Psalms 19-21; Proverbs 4:1-19

Where the Road Leads

Devotional Text: Proverbs 4:18-19

A familiar theme of the Bible is that we have a choice in the direction and the way we will go. Jesus said there are two ways: the broad way that leads to destruction and the narrow way that leads to life (Matt. 7:13-14). The book of Psalms opens by contrasting the way of the righteous and the way of the wicked (Psalm 1).

Now, here in Proverbs, we have the same idea: "But the path of the righteous is like the light of dawn, which shines brighter and brighter until full day. The way of the wicked is like deep darkness; they do not know over what they stumble" (Prov. 4:18-19).

We all are on one path or another. Have we given very conscious thought to which one that is and where it is headed?

FEBRUARY

12

Daily Bible Reading: Exodus 28-29; Matthew 27:1-31

Dabbling in Sin

Devotional Text: Matthew 27:5

None is so infamous as Judas, the betrayer of Jesus. His treachery is much better remembered than his remorse. He was quite sad for what he'd done. But why did he do what he did? What would possess a man to follow this path of betrayal?

We know Judas was greedy (John 12:6), and the reward offered for the betrayal appealed to him. We also know that Judas had witnessed many occasions on which Jesus had escaped traps laid by his enemies, who were intending to discredit and shame Him. Perhaps Judas thought that the same would happen again: Jesus would deftly avoid whatever these men had in mind, and, in the process, he would make some money for himself. No harm, no foul.

Boy, was he wrong. So are we anytime we begin dabbling in wrongdoing, no matter how we might think it's all going to work out (2 Thess. 5:22; Jas. 4:7).

13

Daily Bible Reading: Exodus 30-31; Matthew 27:32-66

Building God's Tabernacle

Devotional Text: Exodus 31:6

During the construction of the tabernacle at Mt. Sinai, God told Moses He had given His Spirit to certain men so that they would be able to possess the skill of craftsmanship in making all of the furnishings and designs for God's tent (Ex. 31:1-11). The intent of all of this was so that "they may make all that I have commanded you" (v. 6).

God's Spirit was also employed when He wanted His word given to men in written form. He guided that entire process (2 Peter 1:20-21).

His Spirit is also to be at work in us because God wants to make something out of us. Just like He had in mind His tabernacle and the Bible, He has in mind a person characterized by love, joy, peace, patience, kindness, goodness, faithfulness, gentleness, and self-control (Gal. 5:22-23).

14

Daily Bible Reading: Exodus 32-33; Matthew 28

Fear and Joy

Devotional Text: Matthew 28:8

Fear and joy are not emotions we typically associate with one another. Yet, when the women left Jesus' tomb on the first day of the week, they were filled with both.

We have no problem with the joy part. That is, we know why they rejoiced at Jesus' being alive and not dead. We know that we have so much over which to rejoice that we should do so always (Phil. 4:4).

Fear is something else. That one we view as a negative emotion. We're uncomfortable with it; we dislike it. Yet, it is the fear of the Lord that is the beginning of wisdom and knowledge (Prov. 1:7; 9:10).

And so it is fundamental to our relationship with God (Eccl. 12:13).

Think about it. We fear what is bigger, greater, stronger, and has the ability to hurt us (Matt. 10:28). Here was Jesus, over whom even the grave had no control. He is to be feared. But, at the same time, He is the loving, compassionate Master whose same power and might has the ability to bless.

Fear and joy!

15
Daily Bible Reading: Exodus 34-35; 1 Thessalonians 1

Jealous or Not?

Devotional Text: Exodus 34:14

Jealousy is not a favorable character trait. The "green-eyed monster" is hurtful and destructive.

Having said that, what do we do with this: "You shall worship no other god, for the Lord, whose name is Jealous, is a jealous God" (Ex. 34:14)? How can what is so bad in us, be so much a part of God's nature that His "name is Jealous"?

Jealousy in us is petty, selfish, and completely unfounded. Jealousy in God is the result of His nature as absolute and sovereign Creator and Lord. Any devotion, service, or worship directed toward any other is completely unwarranted and unfounded. There is no one else who should ever have our allegiance and devotion.

Jealousy is bad when there could rightfully be someone else, but with God there cannot.

16
Daily Bible Reading: Exodus 36-37; 1 Thessalonians 2

Please God

Devotional Text: 1 Thessalonians 2:4

Are you a pleaser? Some people are like that; they are driven by the desire to please the people around them. That's a frustrating way to live, because it just can't be done. You cannot please everyone. Now, that doesn't mean we have no concern for the cares and wishes of others. Instead, what drives us, what motivates the life that we live, is the desire to please God.

Can we do that? Can the great priority of our lives be doing what pleases God above all else? Paul says, "...so we speak, not to please man, but to please God" (1 Thess. 2:4).

Here's a good question: Above all else, whom do I strive to please?

17

Daily Bible Reading: Exodus 38-39; 1 Thessalonians 3

Be Holy

Devotional Text: Exodus 39:30

Among all the minute details of the tabernacle furnishings and the garments and paraphernalia of the priests, there was a crown for the high priest plated with pure gold. On it was engraved "Holy to the Lord" (Ex. 39:30).

One of the major themes evident in the Law of Moses is that of holiness. Much more will be said about it in Leviticus, but here we're introduced to the concept. What is sometimes hard for us to remember is that the basic idea is that of being set apart. Something is set apart for a very specific use or purpose as opposed to other similar things that are for common and ordinary use. So God, by His very nature, is holy.

We can easily see this concept of holiness with the high priest and all the trappings of his work. But remember, we as God's children are to be holy ourselves: "...as He who called you is holy, you also be holy in all your conduct" (1 Pet. 1:15).

The high priest wore a crown proclaiming him and all he did as holy to the Lord. Our crown making the same pronouncement is the conduct of our lives.

18

Daily Bible Reading: Psalm 22-24; Proverbs 4:20-5:14

God's Framework

Devotional Text: Psalm 22:1

Psalm 22 begins with some hauntingly familiar words: "My God, my God, why have you forsaken me?" These are the very words spoken by Jesus on the cross (Matt. 27:46). It's also interesting that a couple of other statements from this Psalm find meaning in Jesus' crucifixion as well. Verse 16 says, "They have pierced my hands and feet," while verse 18 reads, "they divide my garments among them and for my clothing they cast lots."

This psalm really is not about the crucifixion, although it contains prophetic elements that are fulfilled in it.

At least in the case of the opening lines of the psalm, Jesus appropriated words from Scripture to express His experience on the cross, bearing the sins of mankind (1 Pet. 2:24).

It is interesting that He would use God's Word to describe His sense of abandonment by God. Rather ironic, isn't it? But, Jesus knew what He was experiencing was within the realm of God's plan and God's will. So we too, when we struggle and face hardships, may feel abandoned but, like Jesus, can place that experience in the framework of God's will.

19

Daily Bible Reading: Exodus 40; Leviticus 1; 1 Thessalonians 4

Called for Holiness

Devotional Text: 1 Thessalonians 4:3

We mentioned just a couple of days ago in our reading from the Old Testament about how the high priest wore a gold crown inscribed with the words "Holy to the Lord" (Ex. 39:30).

Like them, Paul tells Christians under the new covenant that God's will for us is our "sanctification" or "holiness" (1 Thess. 4:3). That is, our lives should be lived so as to please God (v. 1), which means to do so according to the instructions given through the Lord Jesus (v. 2).

Paul's point here is that a person should control his or her own body in holiness and honor (v. 4) as God has not "called us for impurity, but in holiness" (v. 8).

Now there's something to think about. Holiness isn't isolated to worship services or to certain individuals who are somehow of higher rank than other Christians. Holiness is everyday and for everyone who follows Jesus.

20

Daily Bible Reading: Leviticus 2-4; 1 Thessalonians 5

A Pleasant Aroma

Devotional Text: Leviticus 2:2

It happened three times in yesterday's reading from Leviticus (1:9, 13, 17), and now occurs six more times today (2:2, 9, 12; 3:5, 16, 4:31). What is it that's showing up so often in all these detailed instructions about sacrifices and offerings? "A pleasing aroma to the Lord."

If you'll notice, it's all in connection with burnt offerings and sacrifices made on the altar. Why is it a pleasing aroma? Does God like the smell of burnt flesh?

Hardly.

Instead, the aroma pleases God because it comes as a result of His people's following His will. There is a persistent and pressing need in all of our lives for the examination of our actions and motives.

The chief rival to pleasing God is pleasing self. It can be a real struggle.

21

Daily Bible Reading: Leviticus 5-6; 2 Thessalonians 1

Pray for Each Other

Devotional Text: 2 Thessalonians 1:10

Notice a couple of lists of words from 2 Thessalonians 1. First, there is "vengeance," "suffer," "punishment," and "destruction"; second, there is "glory," "marvel," and "believe." Those are decidedly different kinds of words, describing very different scenarios, yet--according to this text--happening at the same time and prompted by the return of Jesus.

Whether the first or the second list will describe us at Jesus' return hinges upon one's knowing God and obeying the gospel (v. 8). So, Paul says, "[W]e always pray for you, that our God may make you worthy of his calling and may fulfill every resolve for good and every work of faith by his power" (v. 11).

So, let's also pray for each other.

22
Daily Bible Reading: Leviticus 7-8; 2 Thessalonians 2

Servants of God

Devotional Text: Leviticus 7:1

How about today, instead of developing a single thought, we introduce a series of thoughts, or rather a series of words and phrases from Leviticus 7-8? Let these serve to prompt our thinking as servants of God under the new covenant as we observe the servants of God under the old covenant.

Here they are:
- It is most holy.
- Guilt offering
- Peace offerings for thanksgiving
- Serve as priests of the Lord
- Bring their offerings to the Lord
- This is the thing that the Lord has commanded to be done.
- Consecrated them
- Atonement
- Did all the things that the Lord commanded

23

Daily Bible Reading: Leviticus 9-11; 2 Thessalonians 3

Growing Faith

Devotional Text: 2 Thessalonians 3:2

"For not all have faith" (2 Thess. 3:2).

Now there's a sobering thought. It's not that it is a surprise to us. We see the lack of faith and faithless people around us often. But, we also know that "without faith it is impossible to please God" (Heb. 11:6).

And then there's Jesus' haunting question, "Nevertheless, when the Son of Man comes, will he find faith on earth?" (Lk. 18:8).

What about my faith? Is it being fed? Is it being nurtured? Is it being deepened and strengthened?

Reading the Bible every day is a good start (Rom. 10:17).

24

Daily Bible Reading: Leviticus 12-13; Galatians 1

Making Unclean Clean

Devotional Text: Leviticus 12:1-2

Laws for purification and cleansing don't make for the most compelling reading. Though we don't live under that law today, we want to be sure we don't miss the point for us.

People, their garments, and virtually anything they owned could potentially become unclean. That meant, then, that they were not fit for use in worship or service to God. What comes before God or is dedicated to Him, including ourselves, should be as He is: pure and holy.

So, even today, under the covenant of Christ, not Moses, we must lift up "holy hands" when we come to God (1 Tim. 2:8).

It was true under the old covenant, and now also under the new, that what is unclean should be made clean (1 Cor. 6:11).

25
Daily Bible Reading: Psalms 25-27; Proverbs 5:16-6:5

A Good Intoxication

Devotional Text: Proverbs 5:19

Proverbs is all about living wisely: living life so as to avoid common pitfalls, problems, and mistakes while enjoying its greatest rewards and blessings.

A common theme of the book is sex. Like anything that has great potential for pleasure and good, it can be misused and abused so as to become a source of misery and pain. A primary key to achieving the former and avoiding the latter is marital fidelity.

But, even beyond keeping sex within the bounds of marriage, it's staying in love with your spouse: "...be intoxicated always in her love" (Prov. 5:19).

26

Daily Bible Reading: Leviticus 14; Galatians 2

Not to Be Worthy

Devotional Text: Galatians 2:21

What could possibly be worse? Can you imagine the grace of God being nullified or Christ's death being for no purpose (Gal. 2:21)? Wow! Could anything be more of a slap in the face to God?

That is precisely what happens when we believe that right standing with God is achieved through the good we do, through our obedience to the will--or law--of God. When I think I can earn God's favor by my actions (including reading my Bible every day, among other things), there is no place for grace and no purpose for Jesus' death.

So, then why am I concerned with doing God's will...and reading my Bible? It's not so I can be worthy of God's favor but because Christ is alive in me (Gal. 2:20)!

27

Daily Bible Reading: Leviticus 15-16; Galatians 3:1-25

Real Atonement

Devotional Text: Leviticus 16:30

Today, we are back to Leviticus for our "thought." By the way, I don't know if you've noticed or not, but I'm trying to alternate between the Old Testament and the New each day with our daily thoughts. Why? It keeps me from gravitating to the New Testament every day, which would be easy to do. Also, it forces me to look more closely at texts that are not as conducive to a devotional thought (like most of Leviticus). So, we're back to Leviticus.

Chapter 16 instructs about the Day of Atonement. This was when the sacrifices were made for the sins of the people. "For on this day shall atonement be made for you to cleanse you. You shall be clean before the Lord from all your sins" (v. 30).

It's what the Hebrews writer was talking about when he contrasted that sacrifice with the one made by Jesus for our sins (9:23-26). Jesus' sacrifice is a superior one. It was made once for the sins of all mankind.

Our atonement is in the blood of Jesus.

28

Daily Bible Reading: Leviticus 17-19; Galatians 3:26-4:20

Christ Formed

Devotional Text: Galatians 4:19

"...until Christ is formed in you" (Gal 4:19).

That was Paul's goal and intention in working with the Christians of Galatia--and what a goal it is!

Is Christ formed in you? No? No one could make that claim fully.

Not one of us doesn't have room to grow. Not one of us can say, "I have arrived." Not one of us can stand in judgment of another, because we all stand in judgment from Christ.

It's a sobering thought...and a motivating thought--Christ is not yet formed in me. At least not as He will be tomorrow, and the day after that, and the day after that, and...

MARCH

1
Daily Bible Reading: Leviticus 20-21; Galatians 4:21-5:12

Different For a Reason

Devotional Text: Leviticus 20:22-26

Do you like to stand out or blend in? Different personality types have different comfort levels. Some people thrive in the bright lights; others would much prefer hiding in the shadows. Is it being distinctive and unique that has more appeal, or would you rather possess a sameness that draws no attention?

Personalities aside, God wants His people to be different. He wanted the people of Israel to understand that they were unique from other people. God had "separated" them (Lev. 20:22-26). This, He says, defined their holiness.

The same holiness is to characterize the Christian (1 Peter 1:14-16).

When we do God's will, that will separate us from the rest of humanity. We will be a distinct people.

2

Daily Bible Reading: Leviticus 22-23; Galatians 5:13-6:18

Make it Good

Devotional Text: Galatians 6:10

This will be quick: Do good (Gal. 6:10).

God is good (Mark 10:18). Everything He makes is good (1 Tim. 4:4). Everything He gives is good (James 1:17).

All that Jesus did was good (Acts 10:38).

We should do good.

It is the purpose for which we have been made (Eph. 2:10). It should motivate and drive us (Titus 2:14).

Whatever you do today, everything you do today: make it good.

3
Daily Bible Reading: Leviticus 24-25; Romans 1:1-17

God Still Cares

Devotional Text: Leviticus 24:10-16

This is one of those very rare occasions in Leviticus when a narrative is interjected into the listing of laws (24:10-16). It's not a very pleasant story at that. Neither was the one previous to this, the account of Nadab and Abihu (10:1-7). Same thing: people die for lack of adequate reverence for God.

Just because people today aren't being immediately consumed with fire from heaven or being stoned for blasphemy, we should not conclude that this is something about which God no longer cares. He does; He's just handling it differently now (see 2 Pet. 2:9).

4

Daily Bible Reading: Psalms 28-30; Proverbs 6:6-19

God's Glory in Nature

Devotional Text: Psalm 29:2

Psalm 29 is curious. It appears to provide a view of a storm, a particularly violent storm, as a manifestation of the "voice of the Lord."

We sometimes sing:
"O Lord, my God, when I in awesome wonder
Consider all the worlds thy hands have made,
I see the stars, I hear the rolling thunder,
Thy power throughout the universe displayed;
Then sings my soul, my Savior God to thee;
How great thou art! How great thou art!" (Stuart K. Hine)

We quickly recognize God's glory and might in His great deeds in history (creation, flood, exodus, etc.), but He also acts in nature. It's because of this we should, "[a]scribe to the Lord the glory due his name; worship the Lord in the splendor of holiness" (Ps. 29:2).

5

Daily Bible Reading: Leviticus 26-27; Romans 1:18-2:16

More Than Knowing God

Devotional Text: Romans 1:21

Could we ever overstate the importance of knowing God?

Hardly.

As important as it is, it's not enough. Really. Paul described ones that "although they knew God, they did not honor him as God or give thanks to him" (Rom. 1:21). These, he says, are unrighteous and subject to God's punishment.

Alongside our appreciation for the importance of knowing God we must place honoring Him and thanking Him.

For my knowledge of God to be of any worth, I must always concern myself with how I might give Him honor and always give Him thanks.

6

Daily Bible Reading: Numbers 1; Romans 2:17-3:8

God's Promise

Devotional Text: Numbers 1:46

Today's reading gets us started in the book of Numbers. The book's name comes from this event in chapter 1, a census taken of the people of Israel at Mt. Sinai. The total is given as 603,550 (v. 46). That's quite a few folks. But it's only a select group among the Israelites. This was the total number of men, age 20 and older, excluding the tribe of Levi.

Based on the number of this particular demographic of the population, it has been estimated that the entire population of Israelites at Mt. Sinai was probably somewhere in the 2.5-to-3-million range. Now that really is a lot of people.

Remember this all started back with God's promise to Abraham that he would make of him a great nation (Gen. 12:2). That original promise was made to an old man with no children. It hardly seemed possible.

That's how God's promises and assurances are. They may seem hardly possible, but they happen as He says. Always.

7

Daily Bible Reading: Numbers 2-3; Romans 3:9-31

No One is Better

Devotional Text: Romans 3:9

"Are we better than they?" (Rom. 3:9). That's what we want to know, isn't it? Am I better off (spiritually) than that person, or that one? Is the group of which I am a part better off than another group?

Wrong question. Not that the things that may distinguish me from others are unimportant--they can be very important. But Paul's point--and one we should not miss--is that our standing with God is not measured by who is "better" than someone else.

When it comes to one's standing with God, there is one thing to remember: "None is righteous, no not one...all have turned aside...all have sinned and fall short of the glory of God" (vv. 10, 12, 23).

No one is better for everyone sins. But our standing with God is through faith in Jesus Christ (vv. 22, 24). So, though no one is better than anyone else, not everyone has that faith.

8

Daily Bible Reading: Numbers 4; Romans 4

God's Holiness is a Big Deal

Devotional Text: Numbers 4:20

Did you catch what's going on in Numbers 4? In the first 20 verses are instructions for the Levites, particularly the sons of Kohath. When time came to move the tabernacle (remember, the people of Israel are still at Mt. Sinai), it would be the job of these men to carry the objects and furnishings that are in the Holy and Holy of Holy places.

Before they could, though, Aaron and his sons (the high priests) were to go in and cover everything with designated coverings and get it all ready to be moved. The Levites were not allowed to directly touch any of these items or even "to look on them for a moment, lest they die" (v. 20; see also vv. 15, 19).

Wow! Do we get the idea that God was serious about holiness? Not only must He be treated as holy, every aspect of approaching Him--including the physical handling of the ark, the altar, and so forth--were matters of gravest sobriety.

Though God has made Himself so very accessible to us, may that never be translated into flippant or careless attitudes as we approach God boldly (Heb. 4:16).

9
Daily Bible Reading: Numbers 5-6; Romans 5

Bible Reading and Grace

Devotional Text: Romans 5:2

"Through him we have also obtained access by faith into this grace in which we stand..." (Rom. 5:2). We stand in grace.

Grace is favor. We stand, as ones justified by faith (v. 1), in God's favor. That is a new condition. Paul hints at our previous stance when he says we now have peace with God through Jesus Christ (also v. 1). Later he's more explicit, calling us "sinners" and "enemies" (vv. 8, 10); but not anymore.

Being in God's favor--standing in grace--also means we don't deserve to be here. Grace is unmerited.

Here's a thought: why are you reading your Bible every day-- or at least regularly? Is it so that God will look upon you with favor? That won't work. We cannot stand in His favor that way. It cannot be earned. Access into grace is gained by faith.

So, why are you reading your Bible? I hope it is because you are so overwhelmed by God's gracious love that your heart yearns to know Him and His will more perfectly. It's "because of" not "so that."

10

Daily Bible Reading: Numbers 7; Romans 6:1-7:6

Spiritual Leaders

Devotional Text: Numbers 7:1,89

Numbers 7 is long--and repetitive. For every tribe of Israel, a detailed listing is provided of the offerings made. The offering was of items to be used in the service of the Tabernacle that had just been completed (v. 1). The offering was the same for every tribe, and twelve times this list is repeated. Each tribe's offering was given by its leader (or chief).

It may seem detail-ish to us, but something important is happening here. The chapter begins by saying the Tabernacle was completed and consecrated. It ends by saying Moses entered it to speak to the Lord, and he heard a voice from above the mercy seat, "and it spoke to him" (v. 89). In between, the leaders of each tribe acted on behalf of their people with respect to this place that served as the meeting place with God.

Leaders--real leaders--no matter their capacity or duties, will always seek to provide for the spiritual good and well being of those whom they lead. It doesn't matter; parents, bosses, elders, CEOs, teachers--you name it, real leaders have spiritual concerns.

11
Daily Bible Reading: Psalms 31-33; Proverbs 6:20-35

God's Parental Wisdom

Devotional Text: Proverbs 6:21-23

Some people believe the book of Proverbs was originally written for an audience of young men. One of the primary reasons is that so often the teaching is addressed to "my son" or something quite similar. By the time it happens in 6:20, it's already been done fourteen times in this book. Plus, this verse is the fourth time the origin of the teaching is attributed to parents.

Still, the teaching of Proverbs is not just some sort of kindly parental advice to which we politely listen; it is the very wisdom of God (see Prov. 1:7; 9:10). Since this is true, note the "relationship" we should have with God's word:

> "Bind them on your heart always;
>   tie them around your neck.
> When you walk, they will lead you;
>   when you lie down, they will watch over you;
>   and when you awake, they will talk with you.
> For the commandment is a lamp and the teaching a light,
>   and the reproofs of discipline are the way of life" (Prov. 6:21-23).

Though you are reading God's word daily, or quite regularly, is this the kind of relationship you have with it?

12

Daily Bible Reading: Numbers 8-9; Romans 7:7-8:17

Die to Live

Devotional Text: Romans 8:13

Living and dying: it's all very much a part of human existence. We have all been born, and we all, one day, will die. Physically, it happens in that order. Spiritually, though, it is the reverse; we die so we might live.

"For if you live according to the flesh you will die, but if by the Spirit you put to death the deeds of the body, you will live " (Rom. 8:13).

Today you are alive physically, but are you dead? To be alive spiritually, we must be dead "to the flesh."

So don't just be alive today, be dead so you might live.

13
Daily Bible Reading: Numbers 10-11; Romans 8:18-39

Making Something Out of Me

Devotional Text: Numbers 10:33

Numbers 10:33 marks the Israelites' departure from Mt. Sinai. The record of their arrival is way back in Exodus 19:1. They have spent two years here. Now it is time to go and move on toward the land God had promised to give them.

These people are not the same as when they arrived. They came as former slaves, the descendants of Abraham, having escaped the oppression of Egypt. They are now leaving as God's covenant people. They now have a law, a tabernacle, a priesthood, and a sacrificial system.

God had made something out of them. They were now a nation. All that was left was a land that was theirs. And, after a forty-year delay, that would be theirs too.

Remember, God is making something out of us, too (Gal. 4:19). As with Israel, it's not always smooth, and it's not always pretty. Also like Israel, the biggest obstacle in the process is often us.

Let God work, allow His will to be done, and let Him form us to be like Jesus.

14

Daily Bible Reading: Numbers 12-13; Romans 9:1-29

Us Doing or God Doing

Devotional Text: Romans 9:16

There is something to be said for energy, persistence, and work, for putting your mind to a task and getting with it. We admire the person who "takes the bull by the horns" and gets things done.

On the other hand, "it depends not on human will or exertion, but on God, who has mercy" (Romans 9:16).

Before we marshal our resources, set our minds, and expend our energies, time spent in prayer, seeking wisdom, discerning God's will, and identifying His purposes would be a good investment. Let's do what little we can with what little we have in conjunction with the limitless capabilities of God.

15

Daily Bible Reading: Numbers 14-15; Romans 9:30-10:21

At the Right Time

Devotional Text: Numbers 14:39-45

Talk about a major fail; not only had the Israelites not seized the glorious opportunity God put before them to take the Promised Land, they now attempted to go in, without His help, and suffered horrible defeat (Numbers 14:39-45).

Timing, as they say, is everything. The time to do God's will is when He is with you. God calls every one of us to Him to accomplish His purpose. So often, though, like the Israelites, we selfishly act on our own desires, to do what we think and what we want. Then, when we've thoroughly made a mess of things, we decide to do it God's way.

It's not that we cannot come back to Him (remember the Prodigal Son) or that it cannot be done (the people did eventually enter the land). But why not avoid all the mess and the hurt and the heartache to start with? Again, as with Israel, there may be a higher price to pay this time in achieving God's purposes.

The best time to do God's will is when He is with you.

16

Daily Bible Reading: Numbers 16; Romans 11

How We See God

Devotional Text: Romans 11:22

We often see just exactly what we want to see. Our sight and observation are not perfectly objective; they're tainted by our wishes, wants, and desires.

So Paul encourages us to note both "the kindness and severity of God" (Rom. 11:22). I know which of those I prefer. We all like kindness. But God's severity is due to his holiness and perfection. Sin is a complete abomination to Him. "Your eyes are too pure to approve evil, and You can not look on wickedness with favor" (Hab. 1:13; NASB). Come to think of it, I also like what makes God severe.

None of us, beings sinners, could survive God's severity (Rom. 3:23; 6:23). But He is also kind, and through His mercy and grace, we can share His holiness (Heb. 12:10).

God does not change to accommodate us (become one who can tolerate sin, and thus, be no longer holy); He changes us, through His Son, so we might be with Him.

17
Daily Bible Reading: Numbers 17-19; Romans 12

What God Has Done

Devotional Text: Numbers 17:10

Aaron's rod budded (Numbers 17). It not only budded, it had blossoms and ripe almonds. This all came in the aftermath of Korah's rebellion (Numbers 16) and the congregation's continued displeasure with Moses and Aaron.

God intended to make a point. Aaron's rod would be kept in the ark of the covenant as a sign, a reminder (17:10). Aaron was God's man not because he was more talented than others, was able where others were not. It was only because God had put him in that place. Period.

What God has done doesn't have to make sense to us. We may think of something else that seems just as good, or better. We may see no good reason why it couldn't be done some other way. But that's exactly where Korah and his sympathizers were coming from.

Aaron's budding rod is a sign for us too.

18

Daily Bible Reading: Psalms 34-35; Proverbs 7:1-23

Blame or Praise?

Devotional Text: Psalm 34:8

I love Psalm 34. It's one of my very favorites. Maybe it's for selfish reasons.

This person is hurting. He has fears (v.4), troubles (v. 6), is brokenhearted (v. 18), and suffers afflictions (v. 19).

Sometimes, mistakenly, people think the presence of such realities is evidence of a lack of faith. Not true. But notice also what this person did: He sought the Lord, looked to Him, and cried out to Him (vv. 4, 5, 6, 15, 17). He didn't blame God or wallow in self-pity. He went to the Lord for his help and was delivered.

Notice also that now his appeal is to his fellows to join him in praising God, to enjoy the same blessings he's received, to "taste and see that the Lord is good" (v. 8).

Have you suffered or been afraid? Have you sought the Lord and cried out to Him? Have you invited others to join you in praising God and enjoying His blessings?

19

Daily Bible Reading: Numbers 20-21; Romans 13

I Owe

Devotional Text: Romans 13:8

What do you owe? To whom is it owed?

Probably our minds turn immediately to financial debt. Most all of us have some and likely more than we should. There are spiritual implications to financial debt.

The only thing we should owe anyone is to love them (Rom. 13:8). We know God loves us, that Jesus loves us, and that we're told to love each other. But have we thought of loving others in terms of a debt we have to them?

This passage goes on to talk about how loving your neighbor is a fulfillment of the law (vv. 9-10). If you do love, then every one of the law's commands will be honored.

We know we should love God. We owe Him that. Just as surely though, we also owe it to others to love them.

20

Daily Bible Reading: Numbers 22-23; Romans 14

Live So You Can Die

Devotional Text: Numbers 23:10

Balaam is among the most curious of Bible characters. Did God want him to go to Balak or not? Did he not think it odd to carry on a conversation with his donkey?

For all that is uncertain about Balaam, one thing is certain--he never lived up to his intentions: "Let me die the death of the upright, and let my end be like his!" (Num. 23:10).

To die the death of the upright, one must live the life of the upright. Balaam failed on both counts.

Is my goal and intention heaven? Am I living the life now that leads to heaven?

21

Daily Bible Reading: Numbers 24-26; Romans 15

Help

Devotional Text: Romans 15:1-3

The strong must help the weak.

Everyone helps his neighbor.

Jesus has helped us all.

22

Daily Bible Reading: Numbers 27-28; Romans 16

Ever a Leader

Devotional Text: Numbers 27:16-17

Moses would never enter the Promised Land (Num. 27:12-14). He had led God's people from Egypt, to Sinai, through forty years of wandering, to the verge of fulfilling God's promise to Abraham.

Though he would not go in, still he led. He desired for God to "appoint a man over the congregation who shall go out before them and come in before them, who shall lead them out and bring them in, that the congregation of the LORD may not be as sheep that have no shepherd" (Num. 27:16-17).

Moses the relentless leader; Moses the servant of God and His people. Always.

23

Daily Bible Reading: Numbers 29-30; Titus 1

Plan to Join God's Plan

Devotional Text: Titus 1:2

Sometimes I don't know what I'm doing next. I don't prefer to live life that way, but it happens. They call it "flying by the seat of your pants."

Sometimes I know long in advance what I'm going to be doing. That involves planning and preparation.

God has been planning and preparing. Notice: "in hope of eternal life, which God, who never lies, promised before the ages began" (Titus 1:2).

God's planning and preparing His purpose for mankind, began before He even created them. Incredible.

Know that God has a plan, a very long-standing plan, and it involves you.

So here's an idea. Why not make it your plan to participate in God's plan?

24
Daily Bible Reading: Numbers 31; Titus 2

Where Will Others Go Following Your Lead?

Devotional Text: Numbers 31:16

Mystery solved.

Well, sort of. Remember Balaam whom Balak tried to hire to bring a curse down on the Israelites? Balaam wouldn't do it because he said he would only say what God told him to say. But then, Balaam went to see Balak, and God was angry with him even though it looked like God said it was okay to do so (Num. 22-24). That all ends with Balaam saying it wouldn't matter how much Balak paid him, he would not speak contrary to the Lord's commandment.

Shortly after, the Israelites sinned at Peor by playing the harlot with those people, and God punished them (Num. 25). What we didn't know at the time was that all of this was connected.

Here we learn that it was through Balaam's advice that the Midianites seduced Israel and they sinned (Num. 31:16). It appears that Balaam figured out that though it was futile to try to curse God's people directly, he could so advise his suitors to influence God's people to sin and thus bring God's curse on themselves. And that's how it happened.

Balaam's influence led to others' sin. In what direction is my own influence pushing people?

25

Daily Bible Reading: Psalms 36-37; Proverbs 7:24-8:11

You Need to Read

Devotional Text: Proverbs 8:10-11

Sometimes we just need a reminder of how important Bible reading really is.

Our mind knows it. Our heart tells us it's true. But days are busy. Time is in such short supply. We find ourselves at the end of a day...or two, or three, and we realize we've not read our Bible.

Remember, the wisdom and instruction of God's word is of greater value than silver or gold and all that we can desire cannot compare with her in value (Prov. 8:10-11).

So, though no one may be encouraging or pressuring us, and we may not be motivated by seemingly everyone around us doing it, reading our Bible is of tremendous value.

Bible reading is worthy of all the time and energy we devote to it.

26

Daily Bible Reading: Numbers 32-33; Titus 3

Good?

Devotional Text: Titus 3:8,14

How would you classify the activities of your life? What is it that you're doing right now, and why are you doing it? Is it because it's necessary? Helpful? Pleasurable? An obligation?

How about good? How often does "good" register as a reason or motivation for what we do in our lives?

Notice that twice in Titus 3, "good" is precisely the thing to which we are called. Christians should "be careful to devote themselves to good works" (v. 8) and "learn to devote themselves to good works" (v. 14). Additionally, one who belongs to God must be "zealous for good works" (2:14).

I'm not sure what you may aspire to be in life: rich, powerful, influential, happy, loved, or whatever. There's little question about God's aspirations for you. He wants you to be good.

27

Daily Bible Reading: Numbers 34-35; James 1

Provisions From God

Devotional Text: Numbers 35:1-8

The Lord provides.

He has demonstrated that fact time and again as He brought Israel out of Egypt to Mount Sinai and now into the wilderness. Without His provisions, survival would be absolutely impossible. Food, water, and protection, supplied by God, have allowed for this mass of people to live in this hard and inhospitable land.

Now He is making provisions for the tribe of Levi. Forty-eight cities and their pasturelands will be theirs (since they will receive no land as a tribe: Num. 35:1-8).

These seemingly mundane details are but another reminder that God does provide.

And He does so for me.

28

Daily Bible Reading: Numbers 36; Deuteronomy 1; James 2

Partiality Isn't Right

Devotional Text: James 2:8

Partiality or favoritism is a sin (James 2:1-13). God will have none of it in His church.

When we assemble together to worship, think about those to whom we tend to gravitate. There are people to whom we make special effort to speak. We want to be sure and make contact with this one or that. At the same time others are passed by. We may barely acknowledge their presences, if at all.

Why are we selective of those with whom we will share our smiles, attention, and friendliness? Is that not partiality?

The answer is to live by the "royal law," to love your neighbor as yourself (James 2:8). That law applies even when--or I guess especially when--we gather to worship.

29

Daily Bible Reading: Deuteronomy 2-3; James 3

A Blessing, a Curse

Devotional Text: Deuteronomy 2:7

Being blessed can turn into a curse. It really can. When we enjoy riches and comfort and leisure as a result of God's great blessings--and have we not received all of this and more?--what happens when things get a little difficult? All of a sudden life gets more challenging. Do we now struggle and wonder if God loves us anymore?

Coming to the end of 40 years of wandering in the wilderness--think about that for a moment--notice what is said: "For the LORD your God has blessed you in all the work of your hands. He knows you're going through this great wilderness. These forty years the LORD your God has been with you. You have lacked nothing" (Deut. 2:7).

Did you catch it? "God has blessed you...God has been with you...you have lacked nothing."

Shall I complain? Shall I grumble? Shall I question God's love and care for me when things are not just as I would like them?

30
Daily Bible Reading: Deuteronomy 4; James 4

Pleasure or Pain?

Devotional Text: James 4:1

Personally, I prefer pleasure. In nearly every circumstance, if given a choice, I will opt for what is pleasurable instead of painful. Don't you?

Though it may be very natural to do so, it can create a real spiritual problem. "What is the source of quarrels and conflicts among you? Is not the source your pleasures that wage war in your members?" (James 4:1; NASB).

James goes on to say that when our motivation for life becomes satisfying our pleasures, the consequences are quite negative (James 4:3). Such an outlook and approach is selfish and self-serving.

God promises blessing (is that not pleasurable?) to those who deny self and serve others as a higher priority (Phil. 2:3-5).

Pursue pleasure and receive misery; pursue service and receive pleasure. That's how it works.

31

Daily Bible Reading: Deuteronomy 5-6; James 5

A Reminder

Devotional Text: Deuteronomy 5:1

Did you notice what is happening in Deuteronomy 5? It is a repetition of the Ten Commandments. Why would that be? They've already been given once, quite famously at Mt. Sinai.

Think about this. The Israelites are completing forty years of wilderness wandering. That wandering was a punishment for unfaithfulness in wanting to follow counsel of the ten spies who said the people should just return to Egypt instead of going in and possessing the Promised Land. That unfaithful generation has perished in the wilderness. These were the same ones who were at Mt. Sinai. Now, this is a new generation, and they need to be reminded and have reinforced God's will and purpose for them.

Reminders are good. One reason our daily Bible reading is so important is that it provides constant reminders. Just like the Israelites, we need to have God's will for our lives reinforced.

APRIL

1
Daily Bible Reading: Psalm 38-39; Proverbs 8:12-21

The Bible is Real

Devotional Text: Psalm 38:17,21,22

The Bible is real. Not in that it is perceptible by our senses--we can see it and touch it--though we can. It is real in that it is true to life. It deals in reality.

What is not real is television where each program gives us a nice resolution by the end of the allotted thirty minutes or hour. We come to expect that in life, even though that expectation is based on the fantasy world of TV entertainment. Frustration comes with the lack of satisfactory resolution despite the fact that experience tells us that sometimes struggles and troubles are ongoing.

Notice how Psalm 38 ends (and Psalm 39 is no different): "For I am ready to fall, and my pain is ever before me... Do not forsake me, O LORD!...Make haste to help me, O Lord, my salvation! (vv. 17, 21, 22). No resolution, only appeals to God for help.

The Bible's assurance is that reality extends beyond this life. We may get to the end of life and everything may not work out the way we might have liked. But the show's not over. It's in eternity where resolution comes, guaranteed.

2

Daily Bible Reading: Deuteronomy 7-9; Luke 1:1-25

Certainty From God's Word

Devotional Text: Luke 1:1-4

The opening of Luke's Gospel is intriguing. It rarely happens in Scripture that such a candid explanation is given for the original intent and purpose for writing a book of the Bible. Notice several interesting facts that come to light:

- Numerous written accounts circulated regarding Jesus and His ministry at the time of Luke's writing.
- Luke conducted research to learn the facts regarding Jesus' life and work.
- This Gospel appears to have been compiled with an original audience of one in mind, this man Theophilus (compare with Acts 1:1-3).
- This written account by Luke was to provide "certainty" to what Theophilus had already been taught.

We would do well to remember that what is contained in the Bible is there by inspiration. There were uninspired accounts written about Jesus, just as surely as Paul wrote letters that were uninspired (see Col. 4:16 and 1 Cor. 5:9). Though these would be documents of great interest to us, what we have in our possession is what God wants us to know and we need to know. It provides for us the "certainty" we need for life.

3

Daily Bible Reading: Deuteronomy 10-11; Luke 1:26-56

What God Wants

Devotional Text: Deuteronomy 10:12-13

So, what does God want? The Bible is a big book, and God has much to say to mankind. What if it were all just boiled down to a simple, straightforward statement?

Well, it has been, more than once. From today's reading: "And now, Israel, what does the LORD your God require of you, but to fear the LORD your God, to walk in all his ways, to love him, to serve the LORD your God with all your heart and with all your soul, and to keep the commandments and statutes of the LORD, which I am commanding you today for your good?" (Deut. 10:12-13).

Solomon says: "The end of the matter; all has been heard. Fear God and keep his commandments, for this is the whole duty of man." (Eccl. 12:13). Micah says: "He has told you, O man, what is good; and what does the LORD require of you but to do justice, and to love kindness, and to walk humbly with your God?" (Mic. 6:8) Jesus said: "You shall love the Lord your God with all your heart and with all your soul and with all your mind. This is the great and first commandment" (Matt. 22:37-38).

Those are not all different things, but differing expressions of the very same thing.

Now, do it.

4

Daily Bible Reading: Deuteronomy 12-13; Luke 1:57-60

An Unusual Name

Devotional Text: Luke 1:66

John should not have been named John. At least according to custom and expectation. He should have worn his father's name, Zacharias. When both mother and father concurred that his name would be John instead, everyone was astonished.

That, coupled with all the other unusual circumstances surrounding this surprise baby's birth, caused the people to take notice and ask, "What then will this child be?" (Luke 1:66).

That was just it. This child would not be characterized by the usual trappings. He wouldn't wear his father's name. He wouldn't follow his father's trade. He wouldn't even dress or eat like most people (see Matt. 3:4).

This child would be different. As Zacharias had been told by the angel, he would serve a very special role in God's plan (Luke 1:13-17).

So too we, as God's children, are different. We don't think, act, talk, or have the same values as others. As Peter writes, "[A]s he who called you is holy, you also be holy in all your conduct" (1 Pet. 1:15).

People knew John was different. They should know the same about us.

5

Daily Bible Reading: Deuteronomy 14-15; Luke 2:1-20

Helping the Poor

Deuteronomy 15:7-11

Does God care for the poor?

Sounds ludicrous to even ask, doesn't it?

But how does He do so? The provisions of the Law of Moses called for the people to help provide for their needs (Deut. 15:7-11). God helps people through people.

If the needs of the poor are not met, God is not at fault. Are there also people with more than enough to care for themselves? Then God has made provisions: those blessings coupled with His instructions to care for the poor. If there is any failure in this, it with us.

Is it any wonder that Jesus said when we fail to care for the needy that we are failing to care for Him (Matt. 25:42-45)?

6
Daily Bible Reading: Deuteronomy 16-18; Luke 2:21-52

A Light of Revelation

Devotional Text: Luke 2:32

Did you catch what Simeon said? This righteous and devout man whom God allowed to see and hold the infant Jesus and know that this was the fulfillment of all for which He had prepared and planned. He said Jesus was a "light of revelation to the Gentiles" (Luke 2:32).

This statement was actually a quotation of a frequently repeated prophecy from Isaiah (9:2; 42:6; 49:6, 9; 51:4; 60:1-3). What is so interesting about this is that even though it was part of God's plan all along and the subject of much prophecy, the message of salvation being extended to non-Jews became a major issue in the early church (see Acts 10-11; 15; 21:17ff).

Instead of our being critical of these Jewish Christians for their inability to recognize what had always been God's plan and intention, we should ask ourselves if we too might be blind to something God has just as clearly made known in His word.

Lord, help us always to see what you have us to know.

7

Daily Bible Reading: Deuteronomy 19-21; Luke 3:1-20

Why the Cities of Refuge
Are Important For You

Devotional Text: Deuteronomy 19:8-9

This might seem to be a bit of a technical detail, but it is both interesting and important.

God provided for six cities of refuge in the Promised Land. The people were responsible for establishing and providing for these cities. Three cities were to be established initially, then, if God "enlarges your territory...and gives you all the land that he promised to give your fathers...then you shall add three other cities to these three" (Deut. 19:8-9).

After Joshua leads the people into the land and they have taken possession of it, the cities of refuge are listed, and there are indeed six of them (Josh. 20:7-8). That means God had given all the land He had promised according to Deuteronomy. What is more, the text explicitly says, "Thus the Lord gave to Israel all the land that he swore to give to their fathers" (Josh. 21:43).

Why is that important to know? Because so much of what is being said today about the nation of Israel and even the supposed millennial kingdom that will be established on earth when Christ returns is expressly based on the idea that the land promises have yet to be fulfilled. That, according to plain Bible teaching, is patently false.

106

8

Daily Bible Reading: Psalm 40-41; Proverbs 8:22-36

The Bible Reading Way of Life

Devotional Text: Proverbs 8:22-23

Need another reason to read your Bible regularly? Did you catch Proverbs 8:22-23? The instruction of God gives direction, protection, and conversation. It leads us when we walk, watches over us while we sleep, and speaks to us when we wake up.

If we're not consistently engaged with the word, it can do none of those things. How can it talk if we don't allow it to speak as we read it and think on it? How can it lead if we aren't familiar with its wisdom and instruction as we face life's issues and decisions? How can it protect us if our lives are not conformed to its instruction as we submit to His will in all things?

Bible reading is a regular exercise but so much more than a routine. It is the "way of life"!

9

Daily Bible Reading: Deuteronomy 22-23; Luke 3:21-4:13

Highs and Lows

Devotional Text: Luke 3:21

With the genealogy of Jesus interjected between them, Jesus' baptism is followed by His testing at the hand of Satan in the wilderness. In both Matthew (3:13-4:11) and Mark (1:9-13) the events are successive.

Jesus' baptism must be considered a "high water" mark in His ministry. It is typically viewed as the initiation of His public ministry, and what a way to begin, with the very voice of God announcing His identity as the beloved Son and His patent approval of Him. That is starting in style.

Then comes a time of testing and temptation. Though He does emerge victorious, it is a difficult time. It's in the wilderness, and Mark adds that He was "with the wild animals, and the angels were ministering to Him" (Mk. 1:13). This was not an easy time.

So it often happens in our own spiritual experiences. Highs are often followed by lows. A time of spiritual exhilaration is closely followed by a time of spiritual challenge.

We mustn't allow the good times to engender a feeling of invincibility, and neither should we give in to thoughts of despair when we struggle.

10
Daily Bible Reading: Deuteronomy 24-26; Luke 4:14-44

Taking Time to Be Married

Devotional Text: Deuteronomy 24:5

A year-long honeymoon? That seems a bit excessive doesn't it? But it's right there. For a whole year a newly wed man is not to be required to serve with the army or given any other duty but rather to spend that time to "give happiness to his wife whom he has taken" (Deut. 24:5, NASB).

In God's provisions for man's good there is an obvious emphasis on getting a marriage off on the right foot.

It takes time.

It takes effort.

It times concerted attention.

We may not have the luxury today of devoting a year of our lives exclusively to working on our marriages. But, we should devote ourselves always to giving priority to this God-given relationship that can provide some of the greatest blessings and joys God makes available to man.

11
Daily Bible Reading: Deuteronomy 27-28; Luke 5:1-26

So Busy You Have to Pray

Devotional Text: Luke 5:16

Jesus would "withdraw to desolate places to pray" (Luke 5:16).

We know that about Him, don't we? Our Master is a frequent prayer.

Notice what is said immediately before this reference to Jesus' prayer habits: "...great multitudes were gathering to hear Him and to be healed of their sicknesses" (v. 15).

What would we do in that circumstance? If pressed with so much attention and opportunity to do good, would we feel the urgent need for solitude to pray?

Jesus saw an alarmingly great priority in prayer.

That's worth thinking about.

12
Daily Bible Reading: Deuteronomy 29-30; Luke 5:1-26

Why Obey

Devotional Text: Deuteronomy 29:9

The Law of Moses sure contained a lot of laws, didn't it? It is said that Jewish Rabbis had catalogued in excess of 600 individual laws. Deuteronomy 29:9 promises prosperity to the one who keeps "the words of this covenant."

Why would that be? Our first thought may not be the best one. It's not because one who kept God's law in any way created a circumstance that required God to bless them. This prosperity was not an obligation laid on God by faithful obedience.

Instead, God's blessing, as always, is the result of following His will and plan. God's way is best and right. For lives lived in concert with God, it cannot help but "be well for you in everything you do" (Bible in Basic English version).

13

Daily Bible Reading: Deuteronomy 31-32; Luke 6:17-36

Is What I Want a Woe or Blessing?

Devotional Text: Luke 6:12-18, 20-49

Sometimes it's called the "Sermon on the Plain." Jesus had been on the mountain, where He had named the twelve apostles (6:12-16). Now He comes down "to a level place" where "a great crowd...came to hear Him" (vv. 17-18).

This sermon's content (Luke 6:20-49) has many similarities to the Sermon on the Mount and has spawned a fair amount of debate as to whether it's the same or a different sermon. Not that it really matters, but preachers have been known to repeat certain ideas in a number of settings and sermons.

This sermon has its own beatitudes. Here there are four, as opposed to nine in Matthew 5. Also, these four pronouncements of blessing are accompanied by four pronouncements of woes.

At the very least, these are among Jesus' most sobering words. Blessing belongs to the poor, the hungry, those who weep now, and those who are hated, excluded, spurned, and reviled (vv. 20-22). Woe is to those who are rich, full, who laugh, and are spoken well of (vv. 24-26).

Do my desired circumstances elicit from Jesus a blessing or a woe?

14

Daily Bible Reading: Deuteronomy 33-34; Joshua 1; Luke 6:37-49

Still Remembered in Death

Devotional Text: Deuteronomy 34:5-6,8

Short of Enoch and Elijah, two men whom God "took" and did not even allow to die, the passing of Moses stands out as a telling testimony to this great man of God. As per God's plan, he died alone on the mountain where God Himself buried His faithful servant (Deut. 34:56).

A beautiful poem, written by Cecil Frances Alexander, considers this event: "The Burial of Moses." It's easy to find online and worth reading (just do a search of the title or go to: http://www.worldspirituality.org/burialmoses.html). The famed Tennyson said of the piece that it was one of the few poems of a living author he wished he had written. Here is the closing stanza:

> O lonely tomb in Moab's land,
> O dark Bethpeor's hill,
> Speak to these curious hearts of ours,
> And teach them to be still.
> God hath his mysteries of grace –
> Ways that we cannot tell;
> He hides them deep, like the secret sleep
> Of him he loved so well.

The people mourned for thirty days (v. 8). We mourn not just the passing of Moses, but men like Moses--strong yet meek, selfless, fiercely loyal to God's own purpose and will.

15

Daily Bible Reading: Psalm 42-44; Proverbs 9:1-18

A Heart in Turmoil

Devotional Text: Psalm 42:5,11; 43:5

Some scholars believe Psalms 42 and 43 were originally one psalm that at some time and for some unknown reason was divided into two parts. Why would they think this?

Notice 42:5, 11 and 43:5. These verses are nearly identical. They appear to serve as a repeated refrain in a single psalm.

Whether that is all true or not, we should not miss the repetitive point: "Why are you cast down, O my soul, and why are you in turmoil within me?"

The diagnosis, the cure, and the preventative are all the same: hope in God. When we fail to hope in Him, we should expect to be cast down and in turmoil. Trusting in him will bring our hearts to peace and guard them against further distress.

Is your heart in turmoil? Are you downcast?

Hope in God!

16

Daily Bible Reading: Joshua 2-4; Luke 7:1-17

This Impressed Jesus

Devotional Text: Luke 7:6-9

Jesus was not easily impressed. What caught others' attention did not impress Him, and what captured His notice escaped others' (consider His watching as people placed donations in the temple treasury; see Mark 12:41-44).

With a Gentile army officer Jesus was much impressed. He "marveled" at him (Luke 7:9). Why so?

- the man's great faith (v. 9)
- his understanding and appreciation of Jesus' authority (vv. 7-8)
- his sincere humility (vv. 6-7)

This man "got it."

Would Jesus have any reason to be impressed with me?

17
Daily Bible Reading: Joshua 5-7; Luke 7:18-35

The Time to Prevent Ai is at Jericho

Devotional Text: Joshua 7

The battle of Jericho is among the most storied in all of human history. What an incredible event to usher in a new era in Israel's history. Wilderness wandering is behind, and a land flowing with milk and honey lies ahead. The page has certainly turned.

Then Ai.

How can such great victory be immediately followed by inglorious defeat? We learn, of course, it was Achan's sin. He coveted and took the very things God explicitly said were devoted to Him.

What dramatic consequences on the whole nation for the sins of one man. Several points are driven forcefully home:

- No sin "doesn't hurt anybody."
- The innocent sometimes suffer for the wrongs of others.
- We violate God's word to our own hurt and even the hurt of others.
- "Be sure that your sin will find you out" (Num. 32:23).
- The presence of sin will prohibit the progress of God's people.

We only learn from Achan's sin when we make application to our own.

APRIL

18

Daily Bible Reading: Joshua 8-9; Luke 7:36-50

God Forgives

Devotional Text: Luke 7:42

From the perspective of the person who has been good and done right, it's hard to comprehend. Or maybe at least the one who has not done wrong like someone else. Think of the older brother in Jesus' parable of the prodigal son (Luke 15).

What is hard to come to grips with is that the one who has been forgiven much can actually possess a greater capacity to love God. The one who has been forgiven much has done much wrong. He has fallen far. He has travelled further down the path that leads away from the Father.

But God willingly and freely forgives.

So, is the true measure of one's love for God whether he has sinned more or less than others? Remember everyone does sin (Rom. 3:23). Or is that measure taken in terms of how gracious God really is? From how far and how deep He is willing to redeem us?

Jesus' question after telling of two debtors was, "Which of them will love him more?" (Luke 7:42). He further said that Simon the Pharisee had "judged rightly" when he said that the one forgiven more would love more.

Our tendency may be to think in terms of how much less we may have sinned as compared to others. If so, I have become the standard of measure. Instead, we should think in terms of what God has done for us. Then God becomes the standard, and rightly so.

19

Daily Bible Reading: Joshua 10-11; Luke 8:1-21

God's Sun

Devotional Text: Joshua 10:13

The sun stood still. That's what Joshua 10:13 says: "Then the sun stopped in the midst of heaven and did not hurry to set for about a whole day."

So, do you remember science class? Is it the sun that moves in the sky, or does it just appear that way from our perspective on earth? Isn't it that the earth is rotating on its axis while at the same time revolving around the sun? In other words, the earth is doing all the moving.

So, if it really is the earth that stopped rotating, then doesn't that also mean that messed up gravity? It really does just create all kinds of problems with how we are accustomed to the earth and the universe functioning. So, what is the answer to all the problems posed by the sun "standing still"?

Just that God is the one who did it. He's the one who made it all by speaking a word. He caused it all to function perfectly according to the "laws of nature" by which the actions of all things physical are governed. He put it all in place, and it is so precise in its actions that we can send rockets and probes into space to return safely to earth, we can predict with precision the movements of the planets, stars, moons, and other celestial bodies.

If God can speak that all into reality and existence, then He can stop or suspend or do whatever it is He chooses to make the sun stand still and it all not come crashing down.

He can do that.

20

Daily Bible Reading: Joshua 12-13; Luke 8:22-39

Where is My Faith?

Devotional Text: Luke 8:25

"Where is your faith?" (Luke 8:25)

That was Jesus' surprising question for the disciples when they wakened Him during a violent storm on the Sea of Galilee. They feared for their lives and wanted Jesus to rescue them.

Where is our faith? Where is it when we are afraid and consumed with anxiety over situations where we have no control?

Where is it when for so long we've sought solutions to our most pressing problems and none seem to be near?

Where is it when our loved ones are hurting and in pain and we wish for nothing more than their relief?

Where is it when it appears to us that God is not hearing our prayers?

Perhaps we feel as did the father who sought out Jesus to heal his own son. Jesus said all things were possible for the one who believed. To which the father replied, "I believe; help my unbelief!" (Mark 9:24).

April 21
Daily Bible Reading: Joshua 14-15; Luke 8:40-56

A (Old) Man for All Ages

Devotional Text: Joshua 14:9,12

Caleb should be the poster child for the 80-something crowd. What an incredible man.

He showed great faith along with Joshua as one who believed the people of Israel could take the Promised Land precisely for that reason God had promised.

That had been at age 40, and that was 45 years previous.

Now his conviction is that at 85 years of age he can take, as his inheritance, that land promised to him by God for having followed Him fully (Joshua 14:9). Never mind that it is the hill country inhabited by the Anakim with "great fortified cities" (Joshua 14:12).

There were lots of reasons why one might think Caleb could not do what he proposed, the obvious being his own advanced age and the strength of the Anakim.

There was but one reason he believed it could be done: "I shall drive them out just as the Lord said" (Joshua 14:12).

Forget just the geriatric set, Joshua is a poster child of faith for any and every age.

22

Daily Bible Reading: Psalms 45-47; Proverbs 10:1-19

The High Percentage of the Tongue

Devotional Text: Proverbs 10:1-19

Notice how Proverbs 10 begins.

The book of Proverbs is, in reality, a collection of a collection of Proverbs. The first nine chapters are not what we typically think of as far as the structure of a proverb is concerned; that is, two-line statements. But starting here, that "usual" formula is followed.

Out of these first 19 verses in this new section of the book, seven of them have to do with the use of the tongue--that's 37%. And, if you'll take a peek at the next two, verses 20 and 21, they're about the use of the tongue as well (that get's us up to 43%).

If we have any interest at all in living life wisely, in living the life of greatest blessing and that is what the book of Proverbs is all about then we better pay very close attention to the use of our tongues. There is a direct correlation between how we use our words and our speech and the degree of happiness, contentment, and blessing we experience in our lives.

"When words are many, transgression is not lacking, but whoever restrains his lips is prudent" (Proverbs 10:19).

23
Daily Bible Reading: Joshua 16-18; Luke 9:1-17

My Role in Faith

Devotional Text: Luke 9:1-9

Something was going on here.

The miraculous activities of Jesus and His apostles were causing a stir. People had some pretty remarkable theories to explain what they did not understand. Herod was perplexed and curious.

Ideally, the miraculous work of Jesus and His apostles was supposed to lead people to faith. Here we have misunderstanding and perplexity. Had God somehow failed in His intention of bringing people to faith?

Hardly.

We, as human beings, have a role to play in this whole process. God's work and influence is to affect our thinking and understanding. Sometimes our own prejudices and ignorance and faulty thinking gets in the way. It might seem as though God could have chosen another way, but He wants us, as His creation, to play a role. He wants us to make the deliberate choice, based on all He has done, to come to faith.

Could God have done it differently? In a way that would guarantee our faith?

Sure.

But He didn't.

24
Daily Bible Reading: Joshua 19; Luke 9:18-45

Taking What God Has Given

Devotional Text: Joshua 19:51

Today's Old Testament reading completes the account of dividing up the land among the 12 tribes. It began in 18:1 where it says, "Then the whole congregation of the people of Israel assembled at Shiloh and set up the tent of meeting there. The land lay subdued before them."

Already five of the tribes had taken possession of their allotted territories, but now seven had yet to take their possession. Joshua asked them, "How long will you put off going in to take possession of the land, which the Lord the God of your fathers, has given you?" (Joshua 18:3).

That's what chapters 18 and 19 are all about: the last seven tribes being prodded by Joshua to finally take what God had provided.

Amazing, isn't it?

Yes, but not unusual.

Think of all that God promises to give to us as His creation. He wants to provide and bless and overflow our lives with His goodness. Why aren't we enjoying all these good things? Is it because has failed to give? Or it is because we have failed to do what He calls us to do in obedience and living lives of righteousness?

"So, they finished dividing the land" (Joshua 19:51).

Now, do we need to finish our obedience and submission to receive what God gives?

25

Daily Bible Reading: Joshua 20-21; Luke 9:46-62

God's Will No Matter What

Devotional Text· Luke 9:51

Jesus "set his face to go to Jerusalem" (Luke 9:51).

Understand this is a statement of resolve and determination. He knew what awaited Him upon His arrival (see Matthew 16:16-21). It would not be pleasant, to say the least. Yet, it was God's will.

Jesus' life was guided by His goal and purpose which was defined by God's will.

What about your own life? Are you drifting and wandering? Do you know each day where you are going?

True, we may not have all the details, but we can have the determination that we will do God's will, no matter what.

For Jesus, that meant Jerusalem.

What does it mean for you?

26

Daily Bible Reading: Joshua 22-23; Luke 10:1-24

No Matter What Lies Ahead, Be Careful

Devotional Text: Joshua 22:5; 23:6,8,11

We're nearing the end of the book of Joshua and the end of the account of Joshua's life.

He has some solemn things to say to these people whom he has led into the Promised Land and with whom he has experienced everything since Egypt, both good and bad.

It's not hard to understand his emotional ties to them and concerns for what will happen after he's gone.

With that in mind, let's just repeat what Joshua says:"Only be very careful to observe the commandment and the law that Moses the servant of the LORD commanded you, to love the LORD your God, and to walk in all his ways and to keep his commandments and to cling to him and to serve him with all your heart and with all your soul" (Joshua 22:5).

"Therefore, be very strong to keep and to do all that is written in the Book of the Law of Moses, turning aside from it neither to the right hand nor to the left,...but you shall cling to the LORD your God just as you have done to this day...Be very careful, therefore, to love the LORD your God" (Joshua 23:6, 8, 11).

All good advice.

27
Daily Bible Reading: Joshua 24; Judges 1; Luke 10:25-42

One Necessary Thing

Devotional Text: Luke 10:42

What is your schedule like today?

Without knowing for certain, I can guess that it is probably packed, not a lot of free time. Am I right?

Life is just that way. There are so many demands on our time and attention and energy. We feel pulled in many different directions. We would rather it was not like this, but there's not any wiggle room. It's all important. If we left any of it off, we'd feel neglectful.

That's how Martha felt about Mary. She was being neglectful and irresponsible. There were so many chores to be done and duties to be attended to, and Mary wasn't helping.

What she was doing was sitting at Jesus' feet, listening to Him teach.

When Martha complained, Jesus told her that of all the activities going on in that house that day, only "one thing is necessary" and "Mary had chosen the good portion" (Mark 10:42).

So, back to your day. In all that you've done and still have to do, have you given priority to the one necessary thing?

28

Daily Bible Reading: Judges 2-3; Luke 11:1-28

A Very Low Low

Devotional Text: Judges 2-3

Life is sometimes aptly described as a roller coaster, characterized by scintillating highs and frightening lows. The lows can come in a hurry on the heels of highs achieved by long, slow climbs.

The time of the judges is a low, a very low low.

Some of the most fantastic events and colorful characters are found in Judges. It contains more than its fair share of suffering, fear, bloodshed, treachery, and heinous acts.

It's not pretty.

Still, godly people, God's people, remain.

God may, at times, use individuals of less than stellar character. He may allow for events we believe demand His swift and severe retribution.

The time of the Judges is an occasion when stepping back and viewing the big picture provides the best vantage point.

Like the end of a roller coaster ride, the passengers come to their intended place, none the worse for wear.

God will bring His people to their intended place, but for now the ride is a little rough.

29

Daily Bible Reading: Psalms 48-50; Proverbs 10:20-32

What God Wants

Devotional Text: Psalm 50:10,14,23

What does God really want from us?

Is it sacrifices? Is it offerings? Is it worship, praise, and adoration?

In one sense, whatever we give to God, it is already His. That's why the psalm says God won't accept the bull or the goats of sacrifices, because "every beast of the forest is mine, the cattle on a thousand hills" (Ps. 50:10).

No, in our worship we give to God nothing that He needs.

Instead, "Offer to God a sacrifice of thanksgiving" (v. 14).

God wants our recognition of all He has done and does do for us.

"The one who offers thanksgiving as his sacrifice glorifies me; to one who orders his way rightly I will show the salvation of God!" (Psalm 50:23).

30
Daily Bible Reading: Judges 4-5; Luke 11:29-12:12

Threatened by Jesus

Devotional Text: Luke 11:53-54

Can you imagine carrying on a conversation with Jesus?

What would you ask Him? What would you want to know from Him?

And to think there were people who had that privilege but used it in malicious ways.

"As he went away from there, the scribes and the Pharisees began to press him hard and to provoke him to speak about many things, lying in wait for him, to catch him in something he might say" (Luke 11:53-54).

Jesus posed a threat to them. His teaching demanded change on their part. Unwilling to accept that, He, to them, was a threat.

Someday the privilege will be ours to converse with the Savior. How that conversation goes very much depends on our response to His teaching now.

Are we threatened?

"No!" we exclaim.

But are we more interested in submission to His instruction or in staying as we are now?

MAY

1

Daily Bible Reading: Judges 6-7; Luke 12:13-34

What Does God Being With Us Look Like?

Devotional Text: Judges 6:13

The people of God were in a mess. This happened repeatedly during this time of Judges. This time their oppressor was the Midianites.

God, in response to His people's cry for help, called Gideon into service as a deliverer judge. When the angel called Gideon, who like the rest of the people was in hiding in the mountains and caves, he addressed him, saying, "The LORD is with you, O mighty man of valor" (Judges 6:12).

To which Gideon responded, "If the LORD is with us, why then has all this happened to us?" (Judges 6:13). That's a fair question isn't it? It's probably one that we too have asked. Why does all this lousy stuff happen to me if God really does love me and is on my side?

On this particular occasion it had to do with Israel's failure to obey God. Sometimes, that might be our issue as well. We're suffering the consequences of not doing things God's way, and we have ourselves in a mess.

Further, the life we live in this world is filled with struggles and challenges. What God wants us to learn is steadfastness and endurance, and He gives us the power to achieve them (Col. 1:11).

In other words, our present circumstances, as bad as they might be, are no measure of God's feelings or attitude toward us.

God is indeed with us.

2

Daily Bible Reading: Judges 8-9; Luke 12:35-13:9

Prepared Always

Devotional Text: Luke 12:35-40

I was never a Boy Scout, and yet I'm very familiar, as are most people, with their motto: "Always Prepared."

That's an excellent motto for all non-Boy Scouts too. It's a fact that we never do know what is going to happen in life. That being the case, the one who has made preparations before the need or crisis actually arises is in a much better position to successfully navigate these unexpected and possibly rough times.

Preparedness is what Jesus demands of us (Luke 12:35-40). The reason He says we need to be ready is that we do not know when He is coming again.

It continues to amaze and befuddle me that many believers insist that they do know, generally speaking, when Jesus will return, and, therefore, we best get our affairs in order. But Jesus says our readiness is motivated by what we don't know, not what we do know.

Jesus is coming again; we know this. When that will be we do NOT know. It is because we don't know that one thing must be true of us: we are prepared.

3

Daily Bible Reading: Judges 10-11; Luke 13:10-35

The Jephthah Conundrum

Devotional Text: Judges 11:29-40

Oh, Jephthah!

What a sad and tragic story.

People have debated whether or not this account should be taken at face value. Did Jephthah really offer his daughter as a sacrifice to God? It just flies in the face of our sensibilities and everything we know about what kind of thing God likes or accepts.

That's all true. But nowhere does the Bible say anything about God being pleased with what Jephthah did any more than He was pleased with some of the exploits of Samson or others.

Remember, people were doing what was right in their own eyes (Judges 17:6; 21:25). These were bad times; bad things were going on. It was a generation which "did not know the Lord" (Judges 2:10).

Whether we ever go so far as to do something as foolishly rash as Jephthah or as in any of the other sad and unfortunate episodes from the time of the Judges, the real concern is whether or not we know God and are doing what is right to Him.

4

Daily Bible Reading: Judges 12-14; Luke 14

Defied Expectations

Devotional Text: Luke 14:15-25

One thing that can be said about Jesus is that He said some pretty unexpected things.

He didn't follow conventional thought, spit out the standard responses, or go in His teaching where people anticipated He would go.

He gave a parable about a man hosting a big dinner with a big invitation list (Luke 14:15-24). It was in response to a statement from an unnamed person who pronounced blessing on all who would eat bread in God's kingdom.

Jesus knew what people thought about God's kingdom and who would be there. This man's comment was very congratulatory toward himself and all other descendants of Abraham.

The parable taught that the expected guests (those invited) ended up not attending and instead very unexpected guests did: folks from the highways and hedges, that is, anyone who would respond to the invitation. Many of them were poor and crippled and blind and lame.

The application is no less strong for the church. Those who are actually in God's kingdom may very well defy our expectations. They may have something "wrong" with them. They may have needs to be addressed. Their very presence may demand something of me.

God's invitation goes out to everyone. Those who come may not be what we expect.

5

Daily Bible Reading: Judges 15-16; Luke 15

Selfish Marriage

Devotional Text: Judges 16:1-22

Samson and Delilah, one of the great love affairs of all time. Are you kidding me?

Even though that is exactly how this relationship is often thought of, nothing could be further from the truth.

The only thing "great" about it was the magnitude of selfishness in them both.

It's a sad example of what happens when two people come together that are only really interested in themselves. It is absolutely destructive.

Surely this is one of the reasons so many relationships (marriages) suffer so mightily today. When a culture teaches and trains us to be self-centered, self-serving, and self-gratifying to the extent ours does, then we bring two people as products of such influence together in a relationship that is fundamentally giving and "other-centered," can we honestly expect good results?

Romanticizing Samson and Delilah makes no sense. Instead, let's be warned by the horrible and tragic story this is.

6

Daily Bible Reading: Psalms 51-54; Proverbs 11:1-18

Righteous Protection

Devotional Text: Proverbs 11:8

We all want God to help us and to protect us; naturally so.

While we're keenly aware of our desire for that, we may be oblivious to how God actually accomplishes it.

Note these wise words: "The righteous is delivered from trouble, and the wicked walks into it instead" (Proverbs 11:8).

So much of God's protection and help comes in the form of our doing what He says. Sounds simple enough, but think about it. If we're pursuing what is right and associating with those same kinds of people, and trying to steer clear of negative influences and people and situations as much as we can, think about how many problems and troubles we'll avoid.

God has protected so many of His children from the ills and sorrows of drunkenness, for instance, when they have chosen not to drink alcoholic beverages. This isn't even talking about "right vs. wrong" in this regard, but God's help and protection.

We should ask ourselves, just how much do I really want God's help?

Daily Bible Reading: Judges 17-19; Luke 16:1-18

An Abomination to God

Devotional Text: Luke 16:15

"For what is exalted among men is an abomination in the sight of God" (Luke 16:15).

Wow. That's pretty straightforward isn't it?

Of course, it's not an absolute statement; that is, everything that men exalt isn't opposed by God. Is it? Can you not find some people who exalt honesty and integrity and doing good?

Instead, the principle is that following the crowd is a pretty sure way of winding up in the wrong place. Just think about the things that are most admired and valued and pursued in our world. A pretty safe course of action would be to just go in the opposite direction.

The same thing, stated differently, is that "friendship with the world is hostility toward God" (James 4:4, NASB).

The challenge is unending. The influence is relentless. This world, with all it loves and all it exalts, is where we now live.

Lord, may we have the courage to love and honor what you exalt and to shun this world.

8

Daily Bible Reading: Judges 20-21; Luke 16:19-17:10

Foolish Wisdom

Devotional Text: Judges 21:25

Things don't end well in the book of Judges.

The incident at Gibeah (Judges 19) and the consequent dealings with the tribe of Benjamin (Judges 20-21) cast a dark pall over the close of this book.

Then there's the concluding statement, the repetition of an earlier epithet (from Judges 17:6), "In those days there was no king in Israel; everyone did what was right in his own eyes" (21:25).

The depths to which Israel had sunk is measured by the fact that no higher standard of conduct could be found than each individual's own ideas.

What does that say of our own world that promotes individual standards of right and reality as the highest ideal?

"Claiming to be wise, they became fools" (Rom. 1:22).

9
Daily Bible Reading: Ruth 1-3; Luke 17:11-18:8

Ten Percent Thankful

Devotional Text: Luke 17:17-18

Ten lepers received miraculous healing from this dreaded, loathsome disease. Only one expressed gratitude (Luke 17:17).

Statistically speaking, that's pretty sorry numbers. Only 10% were thankful. 10% gratitude.

It's a good thing God's goodness to us is not contingent on our gratitude. That wellspring of blessing might dry up pretty quick.

It's a sad thing if only 10% of the people are thankful. It's sad if we are only thankful for 10% of what God does for us.

Jesus said this man's thankfulness glorified God (Luke 17:18).

How glorified is God by my level of thankfulness?

10
Daily Bible Reading: Ruth 4; 1 Samuel 1; Luke 18:9-34

What God Can Do With Our Nothing

Devotional Text: Ruth 4:13-22

The last name mentioned in the book of Ruth is David. That's David, Israel's great king. He's the great-grandson of Ruth and Boaz. The entire book of Ruth is a testament to the fact that God has and can and does work to accomplish His will. He does so through people, and very often it is through the lives of people for whom life does not seem to have been kind.

Naomi had lost her whole family, except this one daughter-in-law. Her experience had been so difficult she no longer wanted to be called Naomi, but Mara, meaning bitter (Ruth 1:20).

Ruth was at every disadvantage. She was a foreigner (a Moabitess) living among people who mistrusted foreigners. She left her own family and home to follow her down-on-her-luck mother-in-law, Naomi, back to her home in Bethlehem.

From a human perspective, and from Naomi's personal perspective, there just doesn't appear to be much to work with here. Her life and her existence appear to be pointless. It is from that starting point that God begins to work and do marvelous things. It's not because the participants (Naomi and Ruth) have it all together and are on top of their game; far from it.

God's ability to work does not depend on our well-ordered, productive, and smoothly running lives. It just depends on us allowing Him to work.

When our lives get a little messy, don't think it disqualifies us from God's working. As a matter of fact, we may then be most usable by God.

11

Daily Bible Reading: 1 Samuel 2-3; Luke 18:35-19:27

Follower or Blessed?

Devotional Text: Luke 18:35-43; 19:1-10

The blind man would not be denied. When he knew Jesus was nearby, he cried out for mercy. The more people attempted to silence him, the more he cried out. It was his crying out that captured Jesus' attention (18:35-43).

Zacchaeus would not be denied. His diminutive stature would not hinder his being able to see Jesus. It was his climbing the sycamore tree that captured Jesus' attention (19:1-10).

These consecutive events during Jesus' visit to Jericho drive home the point that our determination to see Jesus and be blessed by Him will not be unrewarded.

How many people were in those crowds that followed Jesus? And who was it that was blessed by Him?

It's not enough to just be in the crowd following Jesus. Is your determination to know Him and receive His blessing evident?

12
Daily Bible Reading: 1 Samuel 4-6; Luke 19:28-48

A Wrong Diagnosis

Devotional Text: I Samuel 4:3

A wrong diagnosis can hardly lead to a correct remedy.

Israel had just been defeated by the Philistines. About 4,000 were killed. Their understanding of this loss on the battlefield was that "the Lord defeated us today before the Philistines" (1 Sam. 4:3).

The answer to this problem, as they saw it, was to take the ark of the covenant into battle "and deliver us from the power of our enemies" (v. 3).

It's difficult to tell whether they believed the ark possessed inherent power that would be at their disposal and for their protection or if they believed that having the ark among them would somehow coerce God into being with them.

Either way, the remedy was worse than flawed. It was a horrible tragedy as the Philistines captured the ark and took possession of it. What a travesty!

Back to the diagnosis. It is correct that God was not with them. The remedy for such was not something superficial and artificial like taking the ark into battle like it was some lucky charm or power source. The remedy, as always, was a right relationship with God. God was with His people when they were with him. Due to the poor leadership of Eli and the sinfulness of his sons, the nation was far from God.

They didn't need to bring God to themselves by virtue of the ark, they needed to return to God.

13
Daily Bible Reading: Psalms 55-57; Proverbs 11:19-12:5

That Hurts

Devotional Text: Psalm 56:34

"Sticks and stones can break my bones, but words can never hurt me."

Really? Have we not all been hurt by someone's words? The Bible sure says that words can be very hurtful. They can be "like thrusts of a sword" (Prov. 12:18).

Even so, the Psalmist asks, "What can mere man do to me?" (Psalm 56:4).

The wounds and hurts inflicted by men are very real. They can cause much agony and hurt. Though that may be a reality of life, it doesn't mean we are without recourse. Before asking the question above, the writer says, "When I am afraid, I put my trust in you. In God, whose word I praise, in God I trust; I shall not be afraid" (Psa. 56:34).

Trust in God is the only way we can endure the hurts of men.

14

Daily Bible Reading: 1 Samuel 7-9; Luke 20:1-19

Whose Authority?

Devotional Text: Luke 20:28

This was no mere casual gathering of discontented Jews, like some morning coffee-drinkers' gripe session. In identifying the group confronting Jesus as the chief priests, scribes and elders, Luke lists the three constituent parts of the Sanhedrin. There were no bigger "guns" among the Jews.

Their question was as valid as it was good. They wanted to know by what authority Jesus was doing what He did (He had cleansed the temple; see Luke 19:45-46).

It's a question that still needs to be asked and answered today. By what authority could Jesus claim to be God's Son? By what authority could Jesus forgive sins? By what authority could Jesus demand allegiance and submission?

It is quite telling that these men avoided Jesus' response to their question. They really didn't want to know the answer. They thought they already knew. The reality, though, was that His authority was well established. His authority was greater than their own.

Am I willing to acknowledge Jesus' authority as greater than my own?

15
Daily Bible Reading: 1 Samuel 10-12; Luke 20:20-21:4

Only One Thing To Do

Devotional Text: I Samuel 12:23-24

We think it's a problem when God doesn't give us what we want. For Israel the problem was that He gave them what they wanted.

Their desire was for a king so they could be like the nations around them (1 Sam. 8:5). The real problem here was not that they would have a king; the Law of Moses even contained stipulations for when God's people would be ruled by one (see Deut. 17:14-20). Rather, the critical issue was that in asking for this king, they were rejecting God as their leader (1 Sam. 8:7).

Now, having realized their error, they asked Samuel to pray for them (1 Sam. 12:19).

One of our concerns in serving God is that we would be able to avoid sin (1 John 2:1). Not always being successful with that, another important concern is that we would respond rightly when we do sin.

To that end, Samuel tells Israel that not only would he dare not sin against God by not praying for them, "I will instruct you in the good and the right way. Only fear the Lord and serve him faithfully with all your heart" (1 Sam. 12:23-24).

Israel had their king. And, all of the negative consequences would follow about which he warned them (see 1 Sam. 8:10-18). From this point, though, there was only one thing to do; that was to follow the good and right way.

No matter where we are, there's only one thing for us to do as well.

16

Daily Bible Reading: 1 Samuel 13-14; Luke 21:5-38

Misplaced Trust

Devotional Text: Luke 21:5-6

Jesus' disciples were impressed with the temple (Luke 21:5). They talked about how impressive it was. To them, it represented God's favor and their good standing with God as Jews.

Jesus warned that the day was approaching in which the temple would be so thoroughly destroyed that "there will not be left here one stone upon another that will not be thrown down" (Luke 21:6).

To them, this was unthinkable. What Luke 21 proceeds to record of Jesus' teaching is among some of His most challenging to interpret.

What is not so difficult is recognizing a warning about putting our trust and confidences in the wrong things. Jesus said it shouldn't be in the temple itself. Its days were definitely numbered. Sure, the temple had meaning and significance. But not all that the Jews had come to attach to it. That symbol of their confidence was soon to be destroyed, and then what?

Jesus assures us that there is something in which we can have absolute confidence, and that's His word. "Heaven and earth will pass away, but my words will not pass away" (Luke 21:33).

17
Daily Bible Reading: 1 Samuel 15-16; Luke 22:1-38

God's Regret

Devotional Text: I Samuel 15:11, 35

Have you ever regretted something? Sure. We all have. We have all made mistakes we wish we hadn't, or failed to do something we wish we had. Regrets, unfortunately, are a part of life.

God is said to "regret" having made Saul king (1 Sam. 15:11, 35). That's not a feeling or emotion that we would normally associate with God. It seems to suggest that God made some kind of mistake, and God doesn't do that.

Other translations are not necessarily helpful here either. One even says "the Lord repented that He had made Saul king" (KJV). Isn't repenting something that's done in reference to sin? Why in the world would God ever repent?

This is one of those times when a word in the original language (Hebrew in this instance) poses great challenges to translate adequately into English. Note this comment: "The Hebrew does not express any changeableness in the divine nature, but simply the sorrow of the divine love at the rebellion of sinners." (Keil & Delitzsch, Biblical Commentary on the Books of Samuel, p. 153).

So, the NIV may have the better translation here, reading, "I am grieved that I have made Saul king," and, "And the LORD was grieved that he had made Saul king" (1 Sam. 15:11, 35).

18

Daily Bible Reading: 1 Samuel 17; Luke 22:39-65

Jesus' Habits and Mine

Devotional Text: Luke 22:39

Twice Luke makes reference to Jesus' activities as being His "custom" (Luke 4:16; 22:39). We might say these were Jesus' habits.

And what were they? In Luke 4 it was attending the synagogue service on the Sabbath, and in Luke 22 it was going to garden of Gethsemane for solitude and prayer.

In other words, Jesus' habit was to participate in corporate worship and Bible study (the synagogue was both worship and study) as well as times of private devotion.

You don't have to be a prophet to know where this article is headed.

If these habits were important for Jesus, how much more so should they be for me?

Our lives are filled with routines and habits. They are activities for which a deliberate decision was made at some time and have been so often repeated that they've become nearly second nature. We may have even forgotten the original purpose or intention for which we made the decision about our course of action.

If regular attendance at worship and Bible study along with times of personal devotion are not numbered among our habits, it's time to examine the decisions we've made (or not made) and determine, as should always be true, to follow in Jesus' steps.

19

Daily Bible Reading: 1 Samuel 18-19; Luke 22:66-23:25

The Friendship Investment

Devotional Text: I Samuel 18:1

We all know the value of a great friend.

Either because we've experienced the blessings of such a relationship or we've been deprived of the same.

Surely no greater friendship is to be found in all of the Bible than that of David and Jonathan. "The soul of Jonathan was knit to the soul of David, and Jonathan loved him as himself" (1 Sam. 18:1).

For David, these were exceedingly trying and dangerous times. Were it not for the help and encouragement of his dear friend, he may well have not made it through.

Of all the relationships of our lives, it is that with our friends which can easily be most neglected.

Anything worthwhile is costly. Anything costly demands something from us. Our friendships fall squarely into that category.

Are there friendships in your life that have been neglected? Allowed to diminish due to nothing more than inattention?

Why not make an investment today in something very worthwhile and useful? What friendship needs rekindled in your life?

20

Daily Bible Reading: Psalms 58-60; Proverbs 12:6-24

I Know I'm Right

Devotional Text: Proverbs 12:15

I have a friend I've known for several years about whom I've often thought, "He may not always be right, but he's never in doubt."

Some people always seem to know exactly what to think about every situation. Their thought processes are such that they come to firm conclusions, seemingly about nearly everything.

Though not indicting my friend in any way, it does make me think of this bit of wisdom: "The way of a fool is right in his own eyes, but a wise man listens to advice" (Prov. 12:15).

This is actually a recurring theme of Proverbs. A wise person is one who will seek out counsel, guidance, and instruction and will not rely solely on his own understanding.

"Let the wise hear and increase in learning, and the one who understands obtain guidance" (Prov. 1:5).

"Where there is no guidance, a people falls, but in abundance of counselors there is safety" (Prov. 11:14).

As we formulate our thoughts, ideas, plans, and conclusions, how important to seek out those from whom we may glean insights and wisdom. So, first of all, do you seek counsel from others? And, second, to whom do you turn?

21
Daily Bible Reading: 1 Samuel 20-21; Luke 23:26-56

It's Always Right to Do Right

Devotional Text: Luke 23:35-39

It's hard to do good and right, especially when those for whom it is done are not appreciative or even respectful. The rationalizations to quit come quick and easy.

Maybe it's then that it is most important that we don't quit. Isn't it then that what is good and right is most needed?

Think about Jesus on the cross. Listen to the words Luke uses to describe what Jesus was receiving as He was doing for humanity the ultimate good: "scoffed," "mocked," "railed," and not to mention all while He is being executed in the most vicious manner imaginable (vv. 35, 36, 39).

May we never allow petty annoyances, lack of appreciation, and even outright opposition to ever keep us from doing the good for others we know we should do.

Jesus, as always, is the ultimate example of the teaching: "Do not be overcome by evil, but overcome evil with good" (Rom. 12:21).

22
Daily Bible Reading: 1 Samuel 22-23; Luke 24

Start From Where You Are

Devotional Text: I Samuel 22:1-2

"Everyone who is where they are at, had to begin where they were." Or the saying goes something like that.

The point is, people who are in positions of success and achievement didn't start there. They had to begin somewhere else and work and grow and change to arrive at that place.

When David finally left the house of king Saul for good he "escaped to the cave of Adullum" (1 Sam. 22:1). While there, to this man who would one day become the king over the nation of Israel, the mighty ruler of God's people, men began to gather themselves. "And everyone who was in distress, and everyone who was in debt, and everyone was bitter in soul, gathered to him. And he became captain over them" (1 Sam. 22:2).

A rather inauspicious beginning, wouldn't you say? Not exactly the cream of the crop. But we know what eventually became of David as a leader; and it all began here.

Don't let less-than-ideal circumstances keep you from getting started on what you know you should do or what you can do. Start where you are with what you've got.

23
Daily Bible Reading: 1 Samuel 24-25; Acts 1

Unnecessarily Confined

Devotional Text: Acts 1:1

You probably already know this, but just in case: The same man who wrote the gospel of Luke also wrote the book of Acts, Luke. Though he wrote just two books of the New Testament, he wrote more words in the New Testament than anyone else. Yes, even more than Paul. When he writes, "In the first book, O Theophilus, I have dealt with all that Jesus began to do and teach..." (Acts 1:1), he implies that the book he is now writing, Acts, is a continuation of that same story. This forthcoming record of selected activities of selected apostles is a continuation of Jesus' plan and work.

This is important for two critical reasons: First, Luke is not merely a historian. He is not simply recording what happened to have happened in the birth, development, and spread of the church. The work of Peter, John, Paul and others was by direction of the Holy Spirit. The result was the fulfillment of God's intentional will, not a series of circumstances that could have just as easily turned out differently. What is God's intention for the church and Christian living? We can, and should, look beyond the four Gospels.

Which brings us to the second reason this is so important. To know the will of Christ and follow His teaching, we cannot confine ourselves to Matthew, Mark, Luke and John. The writers of the remainder of the New Testament, the apostles and prophets, were not following their own devices, but rather were guided by the Holy Spirit. Their message was truly Christ's message (see 1 Cor. 14:37; 1 Thess. 2:13; 4:2; 2 Pet. 3:2).

We cannot know Jesus and His word as we should if we confine ourselves to the Gospels.

154

24

Depth of Character

Devotional Text: I Samuel 26:9

Character.

How does one measure character in a person? Certainly one way is to see choices that are made and the motivation for those choices.

When David had an opportunity to kill Saul, there is a line of thought that would completely justify such a course of action. After all, Saul was trying to kill him. Saul had incredible resources at his disposal while David was greatly disadvantaged. And, don't forget the fact that David had already been anointed as the successor to Saul's throne.

But David didn't kill Saul. The reason being that Saul, as long as he lived, still remained the one whom God had anointed. That was reason enough for David to spare his life.

So, we see the depth of David's character. His actions would not be dictated by his personal agenda. It wasn't his own advancement, his own preferences, or even his own preservation that would ultimately guide his actions. God's will, God's glory, and God's concerns would rule David's life.

That's character at its finest.

25

Daily Bible Reading: 1 Samuel 29-31; Acts 3

Needs Over Wants

Devotional Text: Acts 3:6

When we don't get what we want it usually upsets us.

As children we cry and pout. As adults, well, let's hope we've matured some.

Sometimes, though, God actually gives us something much better than what we want.

Isn't that at least part of the message of the crippled beggar in Acts 3? He wanted money, but he got so much more.

Honestly though, was there any reason for him to be asking for anything more than a handout to help him survive? Had he any reason to think that Peter and John could do so much more for him?

Now there is nothing wrong with us asking God for those things we want; how much better when we ask for those things we need the most? We may not even know what those things are.

While we ask God for what we know we want, why not also ask for what we don't know we need?

26
Daily Bible Reading: 2 Samuel 1-2; Acts 4:1-31

Sorrow Hidden or Expressed?

Devotional Text: 2 Samuel 1:19-27

The Bible contains some forms of literature with which we, likely, are not too familiar. Probably the most obvious of these is apocalyptic literature (think of the book of Revelation). With all of its symbolism and figurative language, it can present some real challenges for us.

Another is the lament. By definition laments are expression given to feelings of sorrow, grief, or anguish. It sure isn't that we're unfamiliar with those emotions, but we're just not very adept at expressing them. Many of the Psalms are laments (see Psalm 12; 44; 58; etc.) and, of course, one book of the Old Testament is titled Lamentations.

David penned a lament in honor of Saul and Jonathan on the occasion of their deaths (2 Samuel 1:19-27) and directed that it be published and learned by the people of Judah.

It's been said that the Bible as it is was written for man as he is. I suppose there are many different applications of that axiom, but one certainly has to do with man as an emotional being. We spend much time, and rightly so, talking about truth and facts when it comes to Scripture, but God also has great concern for our emotional well-being.

A lament serves as a healthy means of processing some very powerful emotions. David, obviously, was deeply moved at the passing of his dear friend and his king, even though that king was also his sworn enemy. One can feel his anguish reading these passionate words.

We would do well to recognize and honor our own sorrows and grief as well as those of others.

27
Daily Bible Reading: Psalms 61-64; Proverbs 12:25-13:14

In God's House

Devotional Text: Psalm 61:4

Very similar to the ending of the famous 23rd Psalm, the 61st pleads, "Let me dwell in your tent forever" (v. 4; see Psalm 23:6).

What an honor and delight for one to be able to reside with God. In God's dwelling is found security and safety and blessing.

Psalm 15 poses the question of who may take up residence there. "O Lord, who shall sojourn in your tent? Who shall dwell on your holy hill?" (v. 1). The answer to that question is quite instructive and worth noting.

While on this theme of residing with God, there is the ultimate, as expressed by Jesus: "In my Father's house are many rooms; if it were not so, I would have told you; for I go to prepare a place for you" (John 14:2).

I want to live in God's house.

28

Daily Bible Reading: 2 Samuel 3-4; Acts 4:32-5:16

A Treasured Introduction

Devotional Text: Acts 4:36

Do you remember the first time you met your best friend or your spouse or some other important person in your life? It's interesting to recall that time in which all you knew about that person was what you learned in that initial meeting.

Today's reading introduces us to Barnabas. We are familiar with Barnabas. He's going to play a major role in the life of the early church in Jerusalem, Antioch, and far beyond.

He's going to prove himself to be a great help to fellow Christians at difficult times in their spiritual walks (think of help his help to Saul/ Paul in Jerusalem and to John Mark).

Here, in Acts 4:36, we get our first introduction.

Two things are striking about this; one is that Barnabas is actually a nickname. His mom and dad had named him Joseph. It's the apostles who started calling him "son of encouragement."

Obviously the moniker was deliberate and accurate.

Second, is that Barnabas's desire to help and encourage went to the very depth of his heart. He willingly sold property with the proceeds being used to help the needy. Remember that Jesus said that where your treasure is, there your heart is also (Matt. 6:21).

Barnabas's treasure, and therefore his heart, was with those in need. I'm glad to have been introduced to Barnabas.

29

Daily Bible Reading: 2 Samuel 5-7; Acts 5:17-42

The Bible Interprets the Bible

Devotional Text: 2 Samuel 7:12, 16

An old Bible study maxim says that the Bible is its own best interpreter. Whenever possible we need to allow the Bible to provide the meaning and interpretation of a given text. We're not always afforded that luxury, but sometimes we are.

God's promise to King David that one of his descendants would reign on his throne and God would establish that kingdom forever (2 Sam. 7:12, 16) is a case in point.

Peter refers to this text in his famous Pentecost sermon (Acts 2) and says that based on this promise, coupled with what he wrote in Psalm 16:10, David "foresaw and spoke about the resurrection of the Christ" (Acts 2:30-31).

This promise of God about David's throne played a very important role in the Jews' understanding of the promised Messiah. They knew, and rightly so, that this coming one would be "the son of David" (Matt. 22:42). Thus, the very first verse in the New Testament reads, "The book of the genealogy of Jesus Christ, the son of David, the son of Abraham" (Matt. 1:1).

30

Daily Bible Reading: 2 Samuel 8-10; Acts 6

Should I or Should Someone Else?

Devotional Text: Acts 6:2

It's not right that we should serve widows.

Did I read that right?

Is that not what the apostles in Jerusalem said when addressed with the problem of certain needy widows in the church being overlooked in providing food?

Read it again: Acts 6:1-2.

Well, yes that is what it says, but it's not all that it says.

What wasn't right about it was that they should give up preaching the word to serve tables. It's not that serving tables was beneath them or unimportant. Remember, they gave instruction concerning how this problem should be addressed. But, they needed to devote themselves to what they were best equipped and charged to do.

Here are a couple of important questions:
  • What could I help do that might free someone else to do what they are best equipped and able and responsible to do?
  • What is my primary work and responsibility to which I should give highest priority, as did the apostles?

It's not right that we should ever neglect or forsake our primary work and responsibility even to do some other good and noble work.

31
Daily Bible Reading: 2 Samuel 11-12; Acts 7:1-8:3

The Key is Compassion

Devotional Text: 2 Samuel 12:6

What woke David up? What brought him to his senses?

Throughout all his scandalous affair with Bathsheba, David had been so calloused as to take for himself that which he had no right; to arrange for a failed coverup of his wrong; to order the certain death of an innocent and righteous man. That sounds like a man who cannot be reached.

But he was.

Nathan weaved a tale of the powerful abusing the helpless, of uncaring and blatant disregard for the feelings, much less the rights, of a fellow human being.

It was the lack of "compassion" that outraged David (2 Sam. 12:6; NASB). From there it was but a short accusatory proclamation from Nathan: "You are the man!" (v. 7).

The wretch worthy of death according to David lacked compassion. It's easy to see David's failure. It's not so easy to see our own.

Look at Jesus. Not only how often of Him it is said He had compassion, but also those toward whom it was directed. For instance, "When he saw the crowds, he had compassion for them, because they were harassed and helpless, like sheep without a shepherd" (Matthew 9:36).

We live our lives among "the crowds" of shepherdless sheep. Is compassion our response?

JUNE

1

Daily Bible Reading: 2 Samuel 13-14; Acts 8:4-40

Blessed Problems

Devotional Text: Acts 8:4

Problems aren't always just problems; sometimes they are blessings and opportunities. Two such problems/blessings are introduced in Acts 8:4: "Now those who were scattered went about preaching the word."

Actually, one of these has already been introduced. The persecution that led to the scattering of Christians from Jerusalem is explained in the first three verses of this chapter. Persecution is a problem. But it is also the persecution that led to the spread of the church from Jerusalem to the surrounding environs. We're not told everywhere they went, but we are told of Philip going to Samaria and the results of his preaching there.

There is no reason to think that sort of thing wasn't repeated time and again all over the place as the Christians fled from persecution. The problem became a blessing.

That's directly tied to the second blessing disguised as a problem. Where these Christians went, there was no church (of course not). They couldn't just move into town and identify with the local congregation. Their decision to go or not go to this town or that was not predicated on how strong the church was in this place or whether they liked the church in that location.

What would we do if we moved to a community where there was no body of the Lord's church? What these folks did was take the church with them.

What we classify as problems, might actually be God providing us with great opportunity and blessing.

164

2

Daily Bible Reading: 2 Samuel 15-16; Acts 9:1-31

An Effective, Despicable Leader

Devotional Text: 2 Samuel 15:6

Absalom was a scoundrel. He was a conniving manipulator out to elevate and promote himself at the expense of others, even his own father. He was also very good at what he did. He was good looking, had a winning personality, and was quite persuasive. There's an important lesson to be learned from Absalom.

The Bible says he "stole the hearts of the men of Israel" (2 Sam. 15:6). He did that for his own selfish and malicious ends, but he teaches us something about leading and influencing people.

Is that not something every one of us is trying to do? And don't say no. It is not required that one be in a "position" of leadership. As a parent, as a friend, as a citizen, and as a child of God we are all in a position of influencing other people.

Absalom did several things right.
- He was available (15:2).
- He showed interest in people's needs (15:3). Unlike Absalom, though, our interest should be genuine.
- He showed care and affection for others (15:5).

What Absalom did that was despicable was to undermine his father and suggest that he would not "fail" where his father had. To have actually taken steps to help others in their need would have been the right step.

Absalom's life was a waste of great talent and opportunity for good. Let's redeem some good for ourselves from this wicked man's life.

3

Daily Bible Reading: Psalms 65-67; Proverbs 13:15-14:8

The Problem of Being Blessed

Devotional Text: Proverbs 14:4

During my growing up years I mowed lawns and later hauled hay to make money. Those are good summertime jobs. Winter jobs were more difficult to come by. One particularly unpleasant one was cleaning out the stalls of a horse barn.

Yuck!

I would imagine it is not different than an ox stall. It's a hassle, not to mention a very dirty and smelly job to clean. One way to keep it clean would be to have no oxen. This is precisely where Proverbs 14:4 chimes in: "Where there are no oxen, the manger is clean, but abundant crops come by the strength of an ox."

What is most important is not the cleanliness of the stall, but the crops that come because of the ox's strength in pulling the plow.

Just like in life there are some hassles and undesirable circumstances with which we'd just as soon not have to deal. But are these somehow related to larger and greater blessings?

Being a parent or a spouse or a friend or a member of a church family is not always fun times and pleasantness, but the blessings we can glean from them are far greater than any of the problems we may have to face along the way.

Remember what is most important!

166

4

Daily Bible Reading: 2 Samuel 17-18; Acts 9:32-10:8

What God Can Do and What He Does Do

Devotional Text: Acts 10:4

We need to remember that there is a difference between what God can do and what He does do. Just because He can, doesn't mean He has to or will.

God had taken notice of Cornelius. Here was a remarkable man. He obviously wanted to know and do God's will, and God wanted the same. Notice what God did and did not do. He sent an angel to Cornelius to let him know God acknowledged him and his goodness. What must it have been like to not only see but also hear an angel of God give such an impressive personal affirmation?

But notice, beyond informing Cornelius of God's recognition, the angel told him to send for Peter to "hear all that you have been commanded by the Lord" (v. 33). Why didn't God just go ahead and have the angel tell him what he needed to know?

God's plan is for the saving gospel to be taken by men to men. It's a divine message communicated by human agency.

For people to look for saving experiences outside of the proclaimed message of the gospel is to be looking where God has not chosen to act. It's not that He couldn't; He has simply chosen not to.

Oh, and one more thing; am I allowing myself to be used by God to share Jesus with others whom I encounter who need to hear?

5

Daily Bible Reading: 2 Samuel 19-20; Acts 10:19-48

Deficits and Assets

Devotional Text: 2 Samuel 19:6

Though John Wooden is famous as a basketball coach, he was also a man who understood important, basic principles of life and applied them to the game. One example of this is his saying, "Don't let what you cannot do get in the way of what you can do."

It is easy to focus on our deficits instead of our assets. The problem is that focusing on the negatives, what we don't have or what we lost or what we can't do, is that in so doing we greatly jeopardize the positives-what we do have and can do.

That's precisely what David was doing by the way he mourned Absalom's death. Joab pointed out that David was turning a day of victory over a rebel into a day of defeat. He said it was as though David hated those who loved him and loved those who hated him (2 Sam. 19:6).

Sorrows and regrets and disappointments are a very real part of life. But when they capture our attention or become our focus, then we put at risk all of the good that is also part of our lives.

It would not be wise nor emotionally healthy to act as if the negatives didn't exist, but that doesn't mean that our lives are focused there.

We see the good. We dwell on our blessings and opportunities.

We forget "what lies behind and straining forward to what lies ahead, [we] press on toward the goal for the prize of the upward call of God in Christ Jesus" (Phil. 3:13-14).

6

Daily Bible Reading: 2 Samuel 21-22; Acts 11

The Power and Boldness of Truth

Devotional Text: Acts 11:12

Acts 11 is a good case study in what is right and true overcoming what is not.

Peter was roundly criticized for entering Cornelius's house, teaching those assembled there, and baptizing them into Christ (vv. 1-2).

What these critics had on their side was consensus opinion, years (actually centuries) of tradition, and a majority. All of this no doubt contributed to their boldness in confronting and opposing Peter.

What Peter had on his side was truth.

To know others are with us may be a source of encouragement, strength, and even boldness. But truth and right are ultimately the only things that really do matter.

7
Daily Bible Reading: 2 Samuel 23-24; Acts 12

God's Own Word

Devotional Text: 2 Samuel 24:2

It is an incidental reference, as opposed to a direct and explicit statement.

It serves as a very important reminder of a vital truth. That truth is that the Bible originates with God, not man.

The statement is from 2 Samuel 2:42. "The Spirit of the Lord speaks by me; his word is on my tongue." The thought is consistent with other similar statements in Scripture (see 2 Tim. 3:16 and 2 Peter 1:20-21).

The Bible being God's word makes all the difference in the world. It far surpasses the significance of being great literature, or even the greatest literature. It's so much more than good advice and ancient wisdom.

This is God's word. As such, it carries the weight of absolute authority. It demands something of me far beyond simply my attention.

I am bound by it. I am answerable to it.

Double negative notwithstanding—I cannot not hear, know, believe, and obey.

8

Daily Bible Reading: 1 Kings 1; Acts 13

When God Is With Me

Devotional Text: Acts 13:2,4

The missionary work of the apostle Paul was initiated by the Holy Spirit in a very direct way. It was He who gave direction for Barnabas and Paul (at that time still called Saul) to be set apart for this work (Acts 13:2), and it was He who sent them out (Acts 13:4).

The point here is that this was unquestionably and undeniably a work of God. Yet, on this missionary journey these two men encountered numerous struggles and challenges.

They were deserted by one of their coworkers (Acts 13:13; 15:38). They were run out of town (Acts 13:50). They were threatened with harm (Acts 14:5). And Paul was even stoned and left for dead (Acts 14:19).

If God is behind something, does that mean there will be no trouble or difficulties? God's backing means smooth sailing all the way?

That just isn't true.

So when we face hardships and struggles, we should not make the mistake of interpreting those circumstances to mean we are without God's favor and blessing.

9

Daily Bible Reading: 1 Kings 2-3; Acts 14

My Greatest Wish

Devotional Text: 1 Kings 3:9

In our fantasies we might imagine finding a magic lamp and encountering a wish-granting genie.

It was not fantasy for Solomon, and it wasn't a genie; it was God who said to him, "Ask what I shall give you" (1 Kings 3:5).

The possibilities really do stagger the mind.

Solomon makes an unforgettable request: "Give your servant therefore an understanding mind to govern your people, that I may discern between good and evil, for who is able to govern this your great people?" (1 Kings 3:9).

God was so impressed that Solomon didn't ask for wealth or long life or victory over his enemies that He gave Solomon what he had not asked for: wealth and honor (2 Kings 3:10-13).

What was most important to Solomon, at least at this point in his life, was to successfully achieve God's purpose, and as the king over God's people, that was to rule them well.

What is most important to me? Is it to successfully fulfill God's will in my own life? Rest assured that God will provide (or has provided) all we need to successfully accomplish His will.

10
Daily Bible Reading: Psalms 68; Proverbs 14:9-17

Great Like God

Devotional Text: Psalm 68:5

What makes God so great?

I know that's not really a fair question because everything about God is great. But play along here for a moment. Don't we often think of God's greatness in terms of qualities and characteristics that are so different from us?

God is eternal. He's not bound by time or by space. God is so powerful He can create something from nothing by just speaking. God loves us so much He willingly sacrificed His own Son for us who are rebellious sinners.

That's a short list, but it's a huge list. It could be and is much, much longer.

Notice what Psalm 68 says about why God is so great: "Father of the fatherless and protector of widows is God in His holy habitation" (v. 5). Some of the things which make God so great are precisely the same things He expects to see in me.

Remember James 1:27? "Religion that is pure and undefiled before God, the Father is this: to visit orphans and widows in their affliction and to keep oneself unstained from the world."

God wants me to be like what makes Him great.

11
Daily Bible Reading: 1 Kings 4-5; Acts 15:1-35

A Vastly Important Meeting
Rightly Understood

Devotional Text: Acts 15:28

Our trouble really isn't with knowing what God's word says, but it's with knowing what to do with what it says.

Acts 15 records the events of what is often called the "Jerusalem Conference." Leaders of the early church gathered to discuss and decide on a matter of grave importance for the church at that time--the conversion of Gentiles.

Some have seen this event as justification for church "councils" down through history. These have been given far immense weight in their impact on the church. Such a gathering could never be duplicated in that it involved men directly guided by the Holy Spirit, that is, inspired men (see Acts 15:28).

How should we apply Acts 15? Sometimes brethren do not agree on important matters. It is a good thing to discuss these differences. But most importantly, it is vital that the Holy Spirit provide the answers. In other words, we should be bound by God's own word, which we have, by the Holy Spirit, in the written form of the Bible.

12

Daily Bible Reading1 Kings 6-7; Acts 15:36-16:15

Benefitting From Others' Work

Devotional Text: 1 Kings 6:1

How much of what we do and accomplish in life can we really take credit for? Really?

Are we not indebted to others for what they have done before us? For sacrifices made, for labors and work, for legacies left behind?

Solomon is remembered as the builder of the temple. After all, it was in the fourth year of Solomon's reign that he began to build the house of the Lord (1 Kings 6:1).

While this is true, his father David had made extensive preparations for Solomon's building (see 1 Chronicles 22). He arranged for workers, collected materials, and even charged leaders of Israel to assist Solomon.

Solomon was hardly starting from square one.

We should be careful to not take for granted all of the good things we have inherited from those who have preceded us.

Sometimes you'll hear in certain contexts one saying we are "standing on the shoulders of those who've gone before us." So true.

So first, let's be thankful for the great blessing of others who have made great things possible for us. Then, second, let's take advantage of the great opportunities that are uniquely ours because of those who've gone before.

13
Daily Bible Reading: 1 Kings 8; Acts 16:15-40

Rights, Wrongs, and Salvation

Devotional Text: Acts 16:16

Several things were happening in Philippi that just weren't right.

Some people (we don't know how many) were exploiting a slave girl possessed by a demon in order to make money by her fortune-telling abilities (Acts 16:16). It's not right for the strong to take advantage of the weak and helpless.

The owners of the girl were enraged when Paul cast out the demon from the girl and "their hope of gain was gone" (v. 19). It's not right to value monetary gain above the well-being of another person.

Paul and Silas were unjustly beaten with "many blows" and thrown in prison all because they had helped this girl (vv. 22-24). It's not right to harm and punish those who do what is right.

Not a word is said about all these wrongs. What is emphasized is the conversion of jailer charged with the missionaries' care (vv. 30-34).

This world is full of wrongs. They sadden and sicken us. But it is possible for us to get so caught up in trying to right the wrongs that we miss out on what is most important--salvation!

14

Daily Bible Reading: 1 Kings 9-10; Acts 17

This Queen Had It Right

Devotional Text: 1 Kings 10:1

Jesus was impressed with the queen of Sheba.

She travelled great distances when she "heard of the fame of Solomon concerning the name of the Lord" in order to "test him with hard questions" (1 Kings 10:1).

Jesus said it was her attitude that stood in judgment against the generation of His own contemporaries, because in spite of all that Jesus was saying and doing, they insisted on signs to prove to them His identity (Matt. 12:38ff). "Behold, something greater than Solomon is here" (Matt. 12:42).

Does the queen of Sheba stand in judgment against me?

Am I willing to learn and to know all that God has given and provided so that I might have the faith I should and believe in Jesus as I ought? Or am I thinking that if God would just do this or that, then I'd really be able to believe?

The queen went to great lengths (literally) to do all she could to learn what she could relative to what God was doing through Solomon. That's the attitude I must have with Jesus, the one greater than Solomon.

15
Daily Bible Reading: 1 Kings 11-12; Acts 8

Successful in Business, Successful in Faith

Devotional Text· Acts 18:2

Meet Aquila and Priscilla.

Here in Corinth (Acts 18:1) we gain our first introduction to this Christian couple whom Paul meets through matters of business. They appear to be quite successful business people. They have come from Rome and will later show up in Ephesus (Acts 18:18-19) and, still later, back in Rome again (Rom. 16:3).

Everything we know about this Christian couple is impressive and inspiring.
   • They turned hardship (being expelled from Rome) into an opportunity to do even greater good (Acts 18:2).
   • They housed the evangelist Paul (Acts 18:3).
   • They helped further teach a preacher of the gospel (Acts 18:26).
   • They put themselves at risk for the sake of the gospel (Rom. 16:4).
   • They provided a meeting place in their home for the local congregation (Rom. 16:5).

Aquila and Priscilla did everything they could, wherever they were, to support and encourage and promote the cause of Jesus Christ. They were actively engaged in the work of Lord always and in whatever capacity they could be.

Though they weren't involved in fulltime ministry, they were fully engaged in the Lord's work.

16
Daily Bible Reading: 1 Kings 13-14; Acts 19:1-22

Right to Whom?

Devotional Text: 1 Kings 14:8

God's displeasure with King Jeroboam was great. He sent a prophet to warn him of that displeasure and even provided a miraculous sign to verify that the messenger was indeed from God (1 Kings 13:16). Yet, "Jeroboam did not turn from his evil way" (1 Kings 13:33).

Later God also sent a message by the prophet Ahijah, saying that Jeroboam had failed to do as David who did "only that which was right in My eyes" (1 Kings 14:8).

Contrast that to the assessment of the time of the Judges when everyone "did what was right in his own eyes" (Judges 21:25).

It really is as straightforward as that. Will we do what's right in our own eyes or in God's eyes?

17

Daily Bible Reading: Psalms 69-70; Proverbs 14:18-35

The Way to Honor God

Devotional Text: Proverbs 14:31

Do you remember the confusion at the judgment scene Jesus described when He tells those separated to the right and the left that they either had or had not fed Him when He was hungry, clothed Him when He was naked, and so on (Matt. 25:3146)?

They wanted to know when they had ever seen Jesus in any of those conditions He described. He responded that as they treated "one of the least of these my brothers" who were like that, they did it to Him.

That's a sobering thought. As we treat the needy we encounter, that's how we treat Jesus.

Add to that Proverbs 14:31, "Whoever oppresses a poor man insults his Maker, but he who is generous to the needy honors Him."

Our attitude to the poor and needy is our attitude toward God.

18
Daily Bible Reading: 1 Kings 15-16; Acts 9:23

Paul's Money Trouble

Devotional Text: Acts 19:23-27

Have you ever had money trouble?

No, not the kind where you don't have enough of it to cover expenses. Rather, the kind that Paul encountered earlier at Philippi (Acts 16:16ff) and now again at Ephesus (Acts 19:23ff).

In both of these places, his work in spreading the gospel affected the pocketbook of folks profiting from false religion. In Philippi Paul cast a demon from a slave girl who was being exploited as a fortuneteller. He and Silas wound up beaten and in prison over that one.

Now the effectiveness of the gospel was adversely affecting the sale of images to Artemis in Ephesus, a fact the silversmiths, makers of those images, did not take lightly. A riot incited by these covetous men threatened the lives of Paul and his companions.

The trouble with money is that it can become a hindrance to the cause of Christ. Truly, "the love of money is the root of all kinds of evils" (1 Tim. 6:10). Not only can it become a barrier to people receiving the gospel, it can move others to act as enemies of the kingdom. Paul also adds that because of "this craving,...some have wandered from the faith and pierced themselves with many pangs" (1 Tim. 6:10).

So, again, do you have money trouble?

19
Daily Bible Reading: 1 Kings 17-18; Acts 20:7-38

Where You Stand is Important

Devotional Text: 1 Kings 17:1

Elijah was a prophet's prophet.

In the famous events on the Mount of Transfiguration, Elijah appears along with Moses, speaking with Jesus (Matt. 17:3). Elijah seems, on this occasion, to be representing all of the prophets and prophecy of the Old Testament.

Rightly so.

We gain valuable insight to the key of this man's remarkable life as God's servant in the opening words he uses as he gives a prophecy to wicked king Ahab: "As the Lord, the God of Israel, lives, before whom I stand..." (1 Kings 17:1).

Elijah fully realized he "stood" before God. That is, he was responsible and accountable to God. Fully understanding the implications of that fact, Elijah acted accordingly.

It is just as the writer of Hebrews describes God as the one "with whom we have to do" (Heb. 4:13; NASB). If we genuinely understand that relationship, then we'll have no trouble serving God as we ought.

20

Daily Bible Reading: 1 Kings 19-20; Acts 21:1-36

Bad Things Might Be the Best Things

Devotional Text: Acts 21:4, 10-14

We need to be careful of the conclusions we draw.

The Holy Spirit repeatedly made it very clear that if Paul went to Jerusalem he would there be bound and handed over to Gentiles (Acts 21:4, 10-14). Based on that, brethren strenuously attempted to convince him to avoid going to Jerusalem. Paul would have none of it.

Who was right?

From the brethren's perspective nothing could be worse than for harm to fall upon Paul. From Paul's perspective, far worse things could happen, and he was more than willing to suffer for Christ.

Notice the Spirit did not indicate what Paul should do, only what would happen to him if he went to Jerusalem.

Is avoiding potential harm really always the best course of action?

It's interesting that when Paul went to Jerusalem, exactly what the Spirit said would happen did happen. But it was the very act of his being bound and placed in the hands of Gentiles (Roman soldiers) that saved his life from an angry mob that certainly would have otherwise carried out their intent of beating Paul to death (see Acts 21:27-32).

Again, we should be very careful about the conclusions we draw. Are those conclusions actually influenced by the facts or by our personal wishes and preferences?

21
Daily Bible Reading: 1 Kings 21-22; Acts 21:37-22:29

The Impact of Our Choices

Devotional Text: 1 Kings 21:25

"There was none who sold himself to do what was evil in the sight of the lord like Ahab, whom Jezebel his wife incited" (1 Kings 21:25).

What a reputation to have.

Ultimately, Ahab was responsible for his own actions; "he sold himself to do evil." It should also be noted, though, that he was influenced in that direction by his own father, Omri. About him it's said he "did evil in the sight of the Lord and acted more wickedly than all who were before him" (1 Kings 16:25).

Then, to make matters worse, Ahab married Jezebel (see 1 Kings 16:31). And not to be outdone by his own father, "Ahab did more to provoke the Lord God of Israel than all the kings of Israel who were before him" (1 Kings 16:33).

Sadly, it doesn't end there. Ahab's two sons become the next wicked kings of Israel (1 Kings 22:51-52; 2 Kings 1:17; 3:12), and his daughter marries the king of Judah and influences him to evil (2 Kings 8:16-18). She's the despicable Athaliah who tries to take over the kingdom when her own son, the king, dies and she murders all her grandsons (2 Kings 11:12).

The effect of our influence reaches much farther than we could ever imagine, for good or evil. Ahab is a sad reminder of this powerful principle.

184

22

Daily Bible Reading: 2 Kings 1-3; Acts 22:30-23:35

Inaction is Not Faith

Devotional Text: Acts 23:11

Sometimes people think that since God is in control then they should just sit back and let whatever happens happen because, after all, it must be the Lord's will, almost as if it were a sign of their great faith.

Paul apparently did not think that way.

The very day after God stood at the imprisoned Paul's side and told him to take courage because he would witness to His cause in Rome as he had done in Jerusalem (Acts 23:11), Paul learned of a plot against his life (see vv. 12-16). Notice that Paul took action. He made sure the commander in charge of his care learned of the plot, and he then made arrangements to move Paul to Caesarea under heavy guard.

The plan to kill Paul was thwarted because Paul took action.

Paul did not take God's direct message to him, as unusual as it was, as a sign that He was going to just somehow cause it all while Paul sat back and watched. God intends for us to use the resources, abilities, and opportunities He's provided.

Our faith is not shown by our inaction.

23
Daily Bible Reading: 2 Kings 4-5; Acts 24

Obstacles to God's Blessings

Devotional Text: 2 Kings 5:1

Naaman was a great man (2 Kings 5:1)

Naaman was also a leper (v. 1).

Naaman listened to a slave girl who told of God's powerful prophet who could heal (v. 3).

Naaman heard the prophet's command, but, unhappy with what he heard, he became angry and did nothing (vv. 10-11).

Naaman was still a leper.

Naaman heard the good sense expressed by his servant and obeyed the prophet (vv. 13-14).

Naaman was cured and thankful (vv. 14-15).

Naaman's pride nearly prevented his being blessed by God.

Don't make Naaman's mistake.

24

Daily Bible Reading: Psalms 71-72; Proverbs 15:1-18

I Need Help

Devotional Text: Psalm 71:5-6, 9, 17-18, 20-21

At one time I believed life would get easier as I got older. I was wrong. Life continues to pose challenges and struggles. Advancing age hasn't lessened these.

Don't get me wrong, I'm not complaining. I just now understand the foolishness of my previous thinking. What's more, I see the need for God's help even more as I do get older.

This all seems to be the thought process of the Psalm 71.

"Upon you I have leaned from before my birth; you are he who took me from my mother's womb. My praise is continually of you" (vv. 5-6).

"Do not cast me off in the time of old age; forsake me not when my strength is spent" (v. 9).

"O God, from my youth you have taught me, and I still proclaim your wondrous deeds. So even to old age and gray hairs, O God, do not forsake me, until I proclaim your might to another generation, your power to all those to come" (vv. 17-18).

"You who have made me see many troubles and calamities will revive me again; from the depths of the earth you will bring me up again. You will increase my greatness and comfort me again" (vv. 20-21).

I've seen the slogan, "Old age is not for sissies." I guess it's true spiritually too.

25

Daily Bible Reading: 2 Kings 6-7; Acts 25:1-22

The Faith's Linchpin

Devotional Text: Acts 25:19

Governor Festus described the complaint of the Jews against imprisoned Paul to the visiting king, Agrippa. He said it was all about "points of disagreement...about their own religion and about a dead man, Jesus, whom Paul asserted to be alive" (Acts 25:19; NASB).

In a way, Festus was exactly correct; the whole issue rested upon whether or not Jesus was alive or dead.

That's still true.

Christianity--all of it--stands or falls on Jesus' resurrection from the dead.

Paul went so far as to say that if Jesus is not raised from the dead, our faith is "futile," we are still in our sins, and "we are of all people most to be pitied" (1 Cor. 15:17, 19).

The resurrection is not a sort of optional feature or some quirky side light of Christianity. It is the linchpin.

No resurrection means no Christianity. Period.

26

Daily Bible Reading: 2 Kings 8-9; Acts 25:23-26:32

The Value of Good People

Devotional Text: 2 Kings 8:18-19

Never underestimate the value and worth of good people.

I'm not saying that you would ever do that, but it's incredible what God has been willing to do, or not do, all because of righteous people.

One of the kings of Judah, Jehoram, a descendant of David, was so wicked that he could only be described as one who "walked in the way of the kings of Israel, just as the house of Ahab had done" (2 Kings 8:18).

So what did God do about this wicked king? "Yet the Lord was not willing to destroy Judah, for the sake of David his servant" (v. 19).

Jehoram was seven generations removed from David, yet because of David God preserved Judah. Amazing.

Remember, God was willing to save the excessively wicked cities of Sodom and Gomorrah if Abraham would have been able to find as few as ten righteous persons there (Gen. 18:32).

Sometimes we are made to wonder why God has allowed the wickedness of our own nation to go unpunished. It's not because we don't deserve it, but perhaps it's for the sake of the righteous.

27

Daily Bible Reading: 2 Kings 10-11; Acts 27

Seeing God's Help

Devotional Text: Acts 27:22-24

Sometimes tragedy strikes our lives. We did not anticipate it, we certainly did not want it, but there it is, nonetheless.

Will we make it through? Will we survive? Will our faith endure? Better yet, will God help us?

The answer to the last question is an emphatic "Yes!" Because it is, then we can answer the others in the affirmative as well.

Where the challenge lies for us very often is in how God helps us.

When Paul's sea voyage to Rome ended in a shipwreck, it was a tragedy. Paul had God's assurance that there would be no loss of life (see Acts 27:22-24).

Look at how they survived. Some swam to shore, and others held on to planks and various items from the ship (vv. 43-44). Some people would fail to see God's hand in bringing them all through this incident safely. It appears that very "ordinary" means were used, but He was there.

So it is with us. God's hand in helping us through tragedies may not appear obvious.

Make no mistake; He is there!

28
Daily Bible Reading: 2 Kings 12-14; Acts 28

Ruts, Both Good and Bad

Devotional Text: 2 Kings 13:2, 11, 24

Did you ever get in a rut? Just doing the same thing you have always done and doing anything different seemed almost impossible? These become self-perpetuating patterns of behavior and are often bad.

Several kings of Israel were the descendants of Jehu: Jehoahaz, Jehoash (also called Joash), and Jeroboam (sometimes designated "II" to distinguish him from a previous Jeroboam). The same thing is said about every one of them: they did not depart from the sin of Jeroboam the son of Nebat who made Israel to sin (2 Kings 13:2, 11, 24).

In Judah the kings are, of course, descendants of David: Jehoash (also called Joash--and it is the same name as the King of Israel above and is confusing), Amaziah, and Azariah. The same thing is said about every one of them; they did right in the sight of the Lord, but they did not remove the high places (which were locations of idolatrous worship; 12:2-3; 14:3-4; 15:3-4). They all were good, up to a certain point. But they could have done better.

In both cases patterns of behavior are perpetuated through three generations. Fathers influenced their sons. Bad behavior passed from one generation to the next.

Those kinds of forces are still at work. What are my own patterns of behavior? Are they good or bad? Chances are, those who follow me will adopt them.

The bottom line? If you're going to get in a rut, be very sure it's a good one!

29

Daily Bible Reading: 2 Kings 15-16; Philippians 1

Good Days and Bad

Devotional Text: Philippians 1:12-18

How's your day so far? Is it a good day or bad?

We've all had both. We'd certainly prefer more of the former and fewer of the latter.

Here's a way you can nearly guarantee that to happen.

How so? Think about how you evaluate a day as to whether it's good or bad. Isn't it usually based on whether or not things are going our way? That's only natural.

Look at what Paul did. He rejoiced in the things that had happened to him (Phil. 1:12, 18). Yet, things weren't necessarily going his way. There were people--actually Christians--who were acting out of envy and rivalry, wanting to increase Paul's affliction in prison (vv. 15-17). It seems that would make for a pretty lousy day.

Paul says, though, that in these efforts they were preaching Christ. That is what made Paul rejoice. His measure of a good or bad day was not based on his own feelings or circumstances. It was based on the cause of Christ and the spread of the gospel.

It would appear that the way to have more good days and fewer bad ones is to forget about self and focus more on Christ (see Matt. 6:33).

30

Daily Bible Reading: 2 Kings 17-18; Philippians 2

A Man for the Time

Devotional Text: 2 Kings 18:57

Looking for a hero? Consider Hezekiah.

First of all, remember that Hezekiah became king of Judah at a particularly trying time.

It was during his reign that God finally took action against Israel and "removed them out of His sight" (2 Kings 17:18). That's the description given of the Assyrians coming and destroying their nation and taking them captive. Too long they had disobeyed God, rejected His prophets, and pursued the sinful practices of the nations around them (vv. 7-18).

The trouble is, Judah wasn't much better (v.19).

Then, Hezekiah became king. Listen to this description: "He trusted in the Lord, the God of Israel, so that there was none like him among all the kings of Judah after him, nor among those who were before him. For he held fast to the Lord. He did not depart from following him, but kept the commandments that the Lord commanded Moses. And the Lord was with him; wherever he went out, he prospered" (2 Kings 18:5-7).

Wow; now that's impressive. He was the man for the time.

Who will be the men and women for this time?

JULY

1

Daily Bible Reading: Psalms 73-74; Proverbs 15:19-16:4

A Path of Success

Devotional Text: Proverbs 15:9, 21, 22, 25, 27-28, 31-32, 16:4

We want success. We fear failure.

It's strange how our actions often put us in line with the latter instead of the former, despite what we want.

Proverbs provides wisdom that leads to success, not failure. Even today's brief reading yields several valuable nuggets:

Be upright and not negligent or lazy (15:19).

Chart a clear path for yourself and pursue it (15:21).

Get good advice (15:22).

Remain humble (15:25).

Avoid all "shady" profits (15:27).

Think carefully before you speak (15:28).

Consider seriously all criticisms and reproofs (15:31-32).

Devote all you do to God (16:4).

That's a good list to keep one on the path of success.

2

Daily Bible Reading: 2 Kings 19-20; Philippians 3

Gains and Losses

Devotional Text: Philippians 3:4-6

Have you ever used a tally sheet? Many people have utilized this tool for helping to make a decision. Draw a line down the middle of a piece of paper, title one column as "Pros" and the other as "Cons" and begin making a list under each column. A more informed decision should follow.

Another use of a tally sheet is to track profits and losses. All the credits go in one column and the debits in the other.

Paul used a tally sheet too, though probably not literally, the principle is sure there. He speaks of things that at one time he had counted as "gain." These were accomplishments and circumstances in his life he'd worked hard to achieve. These caused him to be respected and admired by his peers and were a source of personal pride (Phil. 3:4-6).

His "gain" column was handsomely filled.

Then something happened. He moved everything from that column to the "loss" side of the page. Remarkable! What would ever prompt him to do so?

He met Jesus.

That changed everything. Completely.

All that had been gain was now considered a loss (vv. 7-8). His "gain" side of the ledger now contained but one item: "knowing Christ Jesus my Lord." Numerically, the scales tipped toward the loss side of the page, but in value, the single item under "gain" far outweighed it all.

3

Daily Bible Reading: 2 Kings 21-23; Philippians 4

The Tipping Point

Devotional Text: 2 Kings 21:29

God had reached the tipping point. He had put up with so much up till now. For the sake of good people who'd lived before, and even for His own goodness, God had withheld the punishment His people deserved.

Even during the days of the long string of wicked kings in Israel, He had been gracious to the likes of Ahab and Jehoahaz (1 Kings 21:27-29; 2 Kings 13:45). Eventually, though, enough was enough and the Northern kingdom was punished.

Now it was the Southern kingdom's turn. For the sake of David, God had not punished Judah for their sinfulness (2 Kings 17:19). Then came good king Hezekiah. Actually, he was outstanding (2 Kings 18:5). Things were finally headed in the right direction.Then his son, Manasseh, came to the throne. He was every bit as bad as his father had been good (2 Kings 21:29). God had had enough.

The prophets deliver the news that God will "wipe Jerusalem as one wipes a dish, wiping it and turning it upside down" (1 Kings 21:13). It would be a few years before it happened, but God had made the decision: Judah will be destroyed.

The fact that we don't see God's immediate reaction to our sins as individuals, as a church, or as a nation, does not mean we are "getting away with" anything. As a matter of fact, it's possible that God has already decided He's had enough.

Have we reached, or even passed, the tipping point?

JULY

4
Daily Bible Reading: 2 Kings 24-25; Mark 1:1-20

A Sense of Urgency

Devotional Text: Mark 1:10

You have seen the ambulance on the road with lights flashing, siren blaring, and even the horn blasting. Other drivers behave differently in that setting: they pull over to the right and stop, they remain still at stop signs and green lights, they become very attentive to allowing the emergency vehicle to pass.

The sense of urgency affects behavior.

The gospel of Mark has about it a sense of urgency. Though it is more subtle, no sirens or flashing lights, it's still there. It's seen in a word most frequently found in our English translations as "immediately." It's there four times in verses 10-20 of chapter one, seven more times before the end of the chapter, eighteen more times in the next seven chapters, and a total of thirty-nine times in the whole book.

"Immediately...immediately....immediately..."

Mark shows us an urgency about Jesus. And urgency affects behavior.

Urgency creates attentiveness. Urgency leads to action that is not typical.

If Jesus is not urgent to me, my behavior will never change.

Jesus is very much concerned about my behavior, that I "do the things that [He] says" (Lk. 6:46).

5

Daily Bible Reading: 1 Chronicles 1; Mark 1:21-45

A Very Good Reminder

Devotional Text: 1 Chronicles 1:1

Get ready to think to yourself, "I've read this before."

The books of 1 and 2 Chronicles cover virtually the same history as do the books of 1 Samuel through 2 Kings. It's from a perspective much later in Israel's history: that of the exiles returning from the 70 years of Babylonian captivity after Jerusalem had been destroyed.

In the Hebrew Bible, these books are actually located as the last two books in sequence, instead of following Kings as in our English Bibles. The whole purpose of Chronicles is for the benefit of former captives to Babylon and ones whose homeland and beloved Jerusalem lay in ruins. These books are a reminder of their true identity.

So, 1 Chronicles begins, "Adam, Seth, Enosh..." (1:1).

Their identity goes back to the very beginning. The same God who created Adam is the God of their forefathers, who has been with them, despite captivity, down to this very day. So, for the first nine chapters we find an extensive genealogy, from Adam all the way down those who have been in exile.

Knowing we are God's is an important point to know, reinforce, and of which to be reminded.

6

Daily Bible Reading: 1 Chronicles 2; Mark 2:1-22

Faith Seen

Devotional Text: Mark 2:5

Do you have faith?

If yes, how can anyone else know?

We might think that telling them about it would be the best means. And, there would be lots to tell. You could explain what you believe, what you think a person should do or not do; you could talk about worship and salvation; you could just talk about an awful lot.

But that's not the best way for them to know.

Jesus knew about people's faith that didn't say a word. And, no, it's not because of His capacity as deity to know all things. Mark says He knew it because He saw it (Mark 2:5).

This is precisely consistent, as we would expect, with James' discussion of faith (James 2:14-26). The difference between saying and doing is critical. Faith is not what we say or think or believe, it's what we do.

James has a word for faith that is all talk, dead.

7
Daily Bible Reading: 1 Chronicles 3-4; Mark 2:23-3:35

What a Name Means

Devotional Text: 1 Chronicles 4:9

Sometimes names mean something, sometimes they don't.

Why parents give a child a certain name could be for a great many different reasons.

Sometimes it's a family name. Sometimes it's influenced by some great or notable person. Sometimes it's just a matter of popularity. And sometimes it's the uniqueness or novelty that attracts parents to a certain name.

There are times in the Bible when names are intended to reflect a reality. Naomi wanted her name changed to Mara, meaning bitter, because her life at that time was a bitter disappointment to her (Ruth 1:20). The irony here is biting since Naomi means pleasant.

Jabez did not want to live up to his name. It was given by his mother because it sounded similar to the Hebrew word for pain, as his birth had been particularly painful (1 Chron. 4:9).

His prayer to God was to be blessed by Him and kept from harm so he would not suffer pain (v. 10). God granted his request.

Our knowledge of Jabez is quite brief and a bit curious (it's hard to even tell where he falls in the lineage). But what we do know is that he made the choice to seek God's blessing and prayed to Him for that.

God heard and answered Jabez's prayer. For all the things we don't know about Jabez, we do know this; and this is important.

8

Daily Bible Reading: Psalms 75-77; Proverbs 16:5-23

Hurting and Remembering

Devotional Text: Psalm 77:4

As the worn out cliche says, "Been there; done that."

Unfortunately.

"I am so troubled that I cannot sleep" (Ps. 77:4).

Haven't we all?

Right now, it seems like God has forgotten. Right now, it feels like I will never have joy again. Right now, it seems like night will last forever (see vv. 7-9).

But I know better. "I will appeal to this, to the years of the right hand of the Most High" (v. 10).

"I will remember the deeds of the Lord" (v. 11). I will remember all the good that God has done. I will remember that He has always helped His people (see vv. 11-15).

Right now I may be hurting, but I will not be overcome, because I remember.

9

Daily Bible Reading: 1 Chronicles 5-6; Mark 4:1-34

God's Word Working In Me

Devotional Text: Mark 4:26-29

Here's a reminder about why reading the Bible regularly, even daily, is so critical.

Jesus' parable of the growing seed (Mark 4:26-29) attests to the fact that just like the farmer sows seed and doesn't know exactly how it germinates, develops and grows, neither do we know how God's word is able to accomplish its work in human hearts.

The farmer would never have a crop to harvest if he did not first sow the seed. God's word will never produce its intended fruit in our lives if we don't sow it into our own lives by reading and meditating on it.

This parable also applies to getting God's word out there into the world as well. But for now, that word needs to be in us, so through it God can be at work in ways we do not know or understand.

Read your Bible!

10

Daily Bible Reading: 1 Chronicles 7-8; Mark 4:35-5:20

Our Identity

Devotional Text: 1 Chronicles 7

Compelling reading 1 Chronicles 7 and 8 are not. It concludes the genealogical records of each of the twelve tribes. Well, all except for the priestly tribe of Levi.

What's the point?

Remember, 1 and 2 Chronicles were written when God's people returned to their homeland after having been in captivity for many years. These were a people in need of assurance of who they were and from where they had come.

Notice that in the chapters of our reading these genealogies include the tribes of Issachar, Naphtali, Manasseh, and Ephraim. These are all tribes of Israel, the Northern Kingdom.

They had been taken off into captivity by Assyria much earlier than had the tribes of Judah and Benjamin by Babylon. These were a people deeply in need of a sense of identity.

Our need is no less. We are constantly drawn into the world. Our attention and our time and our resources are in high demand from the lives we now live in this age. Remember, our identity does not reside here. Our citizenship is in heaven (Phil. 3:20).

Our family is God's (Eph. 2:19). Our home is being prepared (John 14:2). Our priority lies with God's kingdom (Matt. 6:33).Let's not forget who and whose we are and from where we've come.

11

Daily Bible Reading: 1 Chronicles 9-10; Mark 5:21-6:6

From Pain to Joy

Devotional Text: Mark 5:22-23

I cannot imagine the anxiety and anguish of the father of a gravely ill little girl who begged Jesus to come heal her (Mark 5:22-23).

A ray of hope must have burst into his heart when Jesus agreed and followed.

Did the angst rise again when their journey was interrupted by a woman who reached out from the pressing crowd to touch the hem of Jesus' garment in anticipation of being healed?

Was it a crushing blow when messengers arrived with the news his daughter had died?

I cannot imagine though I know others can. All of this, while in the presence of Jesus.

Of course, Jesus is going to raise Jairus' daughter from the dead. Incredible joy will fill his anxious heart. But until then, he is hurting.

In this life we will hurt. Following Jesus may not change that for now. We may hurt in a variety of ways until the day we die. Being in Jesus' presence does not mean there will be no pain. At least for now.

Of course, the time will come when our hearts will fill with joy inexpressible. All pain, all sorrow, all tears will then be gone.

Praise God!

12

Daily Bible Reading: 1 Chronicles 11-12; Mark 6:7-29

Utilize Others' Strength

Devotional Text: 1 Chronicles 12:32

Don't be a know-it-all.

The fact is, you can't be. Not anyone knows everything.

I don't know if it's pride or stubbornness, but when we're "in charge" or leading we sometimes try to do it all ourselves. Is that really a sign of good leadership? Not at all.

The sign of a good leader is one who utilizes the talent, knowledge, experience, and abilities of those around him.

That's exactly what David did. Of those numbered among David's "mighty men" were men of Issachar who "had understanding of the times, to know what Israel ought to do" (1 Chron. 12:32).

Who is it around me who knows better, understands better, and can do better than I? It's not that they should lead (or maybe they should), but that as a leader I should utilize their strengths for the benefit of all.

13

Daily Bible Reading: 1 Chronicles 13-15; Mark 6:30-56

Frustrated Leader?

Devotional Text: Mark 6:34

Frustration.

That's a feeling I get when reading this series of events from Jesus' life. The demand on Him was constant. Even when He tried to gain some respite, it failed because the following multitudes just would not leave Him alone. Then, He did make it onto the mountain alone to pray for a brief time, that is until the needs of the disciples demanded his attention and presence.

Two things about this scenario come to my mind. The first is the absence of frustration on the part of Jesus. The incessant pursuit of the multitudes and demands on Him are met with His compassion (Mark 6:34). What a powerful testimony to the genuine selflessness of the Savior.

Jesus knew His purpose. He knew why He came. It was to seek and save and serve humanity (Luke 19:10; Matt. 20:28).

The second point is actually prompted by a quote from Colin Powell. This isn't exact, but he said the day people stop bringing their problems to you is the day you have stopped leading them.

We get frustrated handling other people's problems. But when they bring them to us they see us as a help, an answer, a support, or a leader. Jesus was all of that and more.

How Jesus handled the constant pull of friends, companions, and even strangers is something to think about.

14

Daily Bible Reading: 1 Chronicles 16-17; Mark 7:1-30

Thanked and Praised

Devotional Text: 1 Chronicles 16:4

As an example of David's extensive leadership, notice this detail regarding some of the Levites, which "he appointed...as ministers before the ark of the Lord, to invoke, to thank, and to praise the Lord, the God of Israel" (1 Chron. 16:4). It's not only that there were ones ministering on behalf of the people before the ark, but that in doing so God would be invoked, thanked, and praised.

Does this not provide an excellent framework for thinking about our praying? In them we invoke God; that is, we ask God for those things we need and desire. We can approach His throne to "find grace to help in time of need" (Heb. 4:16).

Our prayers aren't just to make requests of God. They are also to thank and praise Him. Do we give as much thought to the thanks we give Him as we do to the requests we make? It is actually "with thanksgiving" that we "let [our] requests be made known to God" (Phil. 4:6).

And what about praise? Of these three components this may be our weakest point. Undoubtedly, God is worthy of our praise, but we may lack the vocabulary and the familiarity with praise. Reading the Psalms might be helpful to become more familiar with the language of praise (Ps. 148 for example).

As David made sure, so should we, that God is invoked, thanked, and praised.

15

Daily Bible Reading: Psalms 78; Proverbs 16:24-17:9

An Accurate Measure

Devotional Text: Proverbs 16:32

How do you measure strength? By what standard are the powerful and mighty identified?

That's a pretty open-ended question; there are lots of ways. Having the ability to lift heavy weights or to exert energy for long periods of time, possessing large bank accounts, and holding positions of prominence and influence are but a few of the better known measures.

How about self-control? That's not a typical measure, but it is a biblical one.

"Whoever is slow to anger is better than the mighty, and he who rules his spirit than he who takes a city" (Prov. 16:32).

This is yet another example that the most important accomplishments in the human experience are not the things that only the few can do, the elite, the exceptional, the "lucky", but the things within reach of everyone.

16

Daily Bible Reading: 1 Chronicles 18-21; Mark 7:31-8:21

I Don't Understand

Devotional Text: Mark 7:37

Ok, I'll admit it; there are times I just don't get what the Bible is saying. Not that I can't understand the words recorded, but rather I don't get the point being made.

For instance, one of the simplest yet most beautiful tributes offered to Jesus is, "He has done all things well" (Mark 7:37). But this statement is made by people in direct disobedience to Jesus.

Jesus had just healed a man who could neither hear nor speak. Jesus explicitly charged the ones who had brought the man to Him, begging that He would heal him, that they tell no one. "But the more he charged them, the more zealously they proclaimed it" (v. 36).

Maybe this is like the times when demons confessed the identity of Jesus and He would forbid them from speaking (see Mark 1:24-25 for instance). Yet, even though Jesus would tell them to stop speaking, what they spoke is recorded.

Curious.

Though there may be some things I don't know about this, there are some things that I do know: most importantly, what they said is true. Jesus does do all things well.

17
Daily Bible Reading: 1 Chronicles 22-23; Mark 8:22-9:13

What I Want

Devotional Text: 1 Chronicles 22:8-9

We don't always get to do what we want to do, do we? We may not even be able to do good things that we know should be done. Though that may disappoint us greatly, it does not have to be the final measure of our lives.

David wanted to build the house of the Lord, but God wouldn't let him. He said that David had been a man of bloodshed, but Solomon, his son, would be a man of rest and he would build the temple (1 Chron. 22:8-9).

Though David didn't get to do what he wanted, plus he did do some things he shouldn't have and regretted, he's still remembered as a man after God's own heart (Acts 13:22), Solomon did build the temple. It was "exceedingly magnificent, famous and glorious throughout all lands" (1 Chron. 22:5; NASB). Yet Solomon also allowed his many wives to turn "his heart away after other gods; and his heart was not wholly devoted to the Lord his God, as the heart of David his father had been" (1 Kings 11:4).

The point is that whether or not we are able to do what we want, we can always have a heart wholly devoted to God. That is the final measure.

18

Daily Bible Reading: 1 Chronicles 24-25; Mark 9:14-32

Help!

Devotional Text: Mark 9:24

The problem is not whether or not I believe. It's whether or not I believe as strongly and as deeply as I should. And I don't.

I'm pretty certain that I'm not alone in this.

That's why the words of the father of the demon-possessed boy resonate with me as he pled with Jesus' for help. "I do believe; help my unbelief!" (Mark 9:24).

Jesus did help the boy, and he helped the father's faith too.

My faith is also helped. But I won't cease to pray, "Lord, help my unbelief!"

19

Daily Bible Reading: 1 Chronicles 26-27; Mark 9:33-50

Using Well What God Gives

Devotional Text: 1 Chronicles 26:6

Stewardship is a common spiritual topic. The principle of using well what God has given us is so important. Typically we think of it in financial or material terms. Certainly it has its application there, but not exclusively.

Our reading in Chronicles introduces us to the family of Obededom. His oldest son was Shemaiah. To Shemaiah were born sons "who were rulers in their fathers' houses, for they were men of great ability" (1 Chron. 26:6). That is, they "provided outstanding leadership in the family" (The Message).

Stewardship applies to our abilities and talents as well as our money and possessions.

Our abilities may allow us to excel in all sorts of endeavors. We may be wonderful leaders, business people, community activists, athletes, entertainers, craftsmen, or top notch in our profession or trade.

That's all well and good and appropriate. But the sons of Shemaiah applied their great abilities to leading their families. That's exceptional.

20

Daily Bible Reading: 1 Chronicles 28-29; Mark 10:1-31

How God's Love Works

Devotional Text: Mark 10:17, 21

To hear some (maybe most) people talk about the love of God, it is as though God accepts and approves everything about them. He must, because He loves me. Right?

Is that how God's love works?

The Bible explicitly says Jesus loved the man who came to Him that wanted to know what to do to inherit eternal life (Mark 10:17, 21). What Jesus told him was not what the man wanted to hear. The man actually went away from Jesus disheartened and sorrowful because he was unwilling to do what Jesus said he must do (v. 22).

Jesus' love for him did not mean everything about him was acceptable, because it wasn't.

The deciding factor here is not whether or not God loves us, He does. He gave everything for us. Rather, it's whether or not we'll give everything for Him: our will, our life, our possessions. In other words, He loves us, but do we love Him?

21

Daily Bible Reading: 2 Chronicles 1-3; Mark 10:32-52

Is God Impressed?

Devotional Text: 2 Chronicles 1:7-13

God is not easily impressed. I mean, seriously.

Solomon impressed Him. He requested wisdom when God offered him anything he wanted (2 Chron. 1:7-13). He asked for what he knew he would need in order to do what God called Him to do. God liked that.

What has God called us to do? Think about that for a moment, as a Christian, a spouse, a child, a citizen, an employee, a friend, etc.?

Have you asked God to help you with what He wants you to do?

No telling what God will give us when we ask Him for what we need to do what He's called us to do.

22

Daily Bible Reading: Psalms 79-81; Proverbs 17:10-28

How Long?

Devotional Text: Psalm 79:5

"How long, O Lord?" has to go down as one of the great questions in the Bible, if for no other reason than its frequency. In just the Psalms alone it is found here in 79:5 as well as 13:1, 74:10, and 89:46. Add to that Habakkuk 1:2, Zechariah 1:12, and Revelation 6:10.

All instances are in the same general context; God's justice seems to be suspended. The righteous and innocent are suffering and/ or the wicked are not being punished. Mankind wants to know when God is going to right the wrongs. How long will it be?

The presence of that question-in Scripture and our own minds-should remind of us of two important realities. First, injustice does exist in this world. We don't like it. It's upsetting. But it is also a reality. It always has been.

Second, God has done and will do something about it, though not necessarily to our satisfaction. Ultimately, God's justice will come at the judgment, at which time we will all want and need mercy, not justice. Even so, every wrong will be made right.

As long as time lasts, injustices will remain and people will ask, "How long, O Lord?".

23

Daily Bible Reading: 2 Chronicles 4-6; Mark 11:1-26

Meeting the Lord's Need

Devotional Text: Mark 11:16

The so-called "Passion Week" was about to commence with Jesus' "triumphal entry" into Jerusalem. The incredible series of events over the coming seven days would culminate in the greatest events in human history: Jesus' death, burial, and resurrection.

Not to be lost in all of that is a simple, yet profound act. Jesus sent two disciples into a neighboring village to retrieve a colt for His use. He warned them they would be questioned about their untying and taking the colt. Their response was to be, "The Lord has need of it." That's it.

Sure enough, it happened just like Jesus said, and when the colt's owners heard the disciples' reason for taking their animal, "they gave them permission" (Mark 11:16).

The colt's owners proved Jesus to be their Lord because they needed no other reason to offer their property for His use than to know His need.

Jesus is my Lord, not based on what I say, but on my response when He has need of what I have.

24

Daily Bible Reading: 2 Chronicles 7-9; Mark 11:27-12:12

For God is Good

Devotional Text: 2 Chronicles 7:1

It's hard to fathom the dedication of Solomon's temple, from the magnificence of the structure and its furnishings, to the pageantry of the dedication ceremony, to the ark's being brought into the Holy of Holies, to the cloud engulfing the temple (as visible evidence of God's glory), to the innumerable sacrifices prepared, to the solemn and inspiring prayer of Solomon (2 Chron. 5-6).

Then, of course, was God's response to all of this. After Solomon's prayer, "fire came down from heaven and consumed the burnt offering and the sacrifices and the glory of the Lord filled the temple" (2 Chron. 7:1). Incredible.

To that the people reacted by bowing down their faces to the ground and worshiped and gave thanks to the Lord saying, "For he is good, for his steadfast love endures forever" (2 Chron. 7:3).

These had also been the words of the Levitical singers when priests brought the ark into the Holy of Holies (2 Chron. 5:13). It had also been part of the psalm of praise David assigned when the he had brought the ark to Jerusalem (1 Chron. 16:34). They would be heard again years later when, after the Babylonian captivity, the temple began to be rebuilt and the foundation was laid (Ezra 3:11; see also Ps. 100:5; Jer. 33:11).

Great words of praise to God who is near in His temple and whose temple now are we (1 Cor. 6:19): "For He is good, for His steadfast love endures forever."

25

Daily Bible Reading: 2 Chronicles 10-12; Mark 12:13-27

What Scripture Says

Devotional Text: Mark 12:24

Hypothetical nonsense: a contrived scenario or situation that appears to make the statement of Scripture impossible.

That's exactly what the Sadducees posed to Jesus (Mark 12:18-27). It's been around for a long time and no less so today. There are many, but the most frequent ones I encounter have to do with why baptism cannot in any way be necessary for salvation.

Jesus said they were "wrong" and knew "neither the Scriptures nor the power of God" (v. 24). What is more, the truth they missed and the Scripture Jesus cited as evidence for it aren't even an explicit statement. Jesus draws an inference from what Scripture says and chastises these individuals for failing to do the same [that is itself an important lesson about how we should approach Scripture to understand it, but that's for another time].

If nothing else, this should serve as a stern warning against drawing conclusions about biblical truth based on our own thinking and reasoning rather than on what Scripture actually says.

It also provides a response to hypothetical nonsense today, our own and that of others.

26

Daily Bible Reading: 2 Chronicles 13-15; Mark 12:28-44

Help For the Weak

Devotional Text: 2 Chronicles 14:11

We love an underdog. We cheer the unlikely victor over a superior opponent: the little guy beating the big bully, the weak overcoming the strong. You know, the proverbial David versus Goliath.

We like underdogs, we just don't want to be one. It's understandable. No one wants to operate from a position of weakness, of disadvantage, of inferiority.

It's certainly not that we would ever choose this position or vantage point, but if we do find ourselves there, do we hesitate to make a move because of it?

Consider King Asa, perhaps the most underrated king in Judah's history. He had an army over 500,000 strong, but the invading Ethiopians' army exceeded 1,000,000.

Asa did not cower in fear, nor was he paralyzed by his apparent weakness. Hear his prayer: "LORD, there is no one besides You to help in the battle between the powerful and those who have no strength; so help us, O LORD our God, for we trust in You, and in Your name have come against this multitude" (2 Chron. 14:11).

God helps those who are weak. If we can only act when we are strong, where is God's help?

27

Daily Bible Reading: 2 Chronicles 16-18; Mark 13

Stick to the Truth

Devotional Text: Mark 13:5

"See that no-one leads you astray" (Mark 13:5). I guess Jesus was not aware that truth is not absolute or that every idea and thought is equally valid. Or that the ultimate "nono" is to suggest someone may be incorrect in their thinking, beliefs, or actions.

If Jesus' warning is valid, then there is truth and reality for which we should strive and from which we must not vary. Also, it is possible for one to pursue a path of thought and action that has dire consequences.

Not surprising, then, is the repeated appearance of similar warnings in the Bible:
- "Do not let your prophets and your diviners
  who are among you deceive you..." (Jeremiah 29:8)
- "Let no one deceive you with empty words..."
  (Ephesians 5:6)
- "See to it that no one takes you captive by philosophy
  and empty deceit..." (Colossians 2:8)
- "Little children, let no one deceive you" (1 John 3:7)

This is not to say that our acceptance by God is determined by our ability to arrive at truth to a greater degree of accuracy than do others. Still, truth is essential to salvation (John 8:32; 1 Tim. 2:4), and we must be cautious of being led astray.

When it comes to notions of truth, whether it's a mere principle encompassing whatever idea or notion one might embrace or whether it is an absolute reality from which we must not stray I believe I will stick with Jesus.

JULY

28

Daily Bible Reading: 2 Chronicles 19-21; Mark 14:1-26

After the Wrong

Devotional Text: 2 Chronicles 19:2

So, it's not a question of whether or not we've erred, because we all have. The question is what we do in response to that sin. Three possibilities exist. One response is wrong (deny or ignore the wrong), and two are correct (both acknowledge the wrong); two are spiritually damaging, and one is spiritually healthy.

So, yes, that means one possible response acknowledges the wrong, but it's still spiritually damaging.

Have you ever known anyone, perhaps even yourself, who readily acknowledged a wrong done, but then believed that somehow rendered them worthless to God's service? The acknowledgment was right, the implication drawn is wrong.

God sent Jehu the seer to rebuke king Jehoshaphat for his wrong (2 Chron. 19:2). To his credit, Jehoshaphat did not deny, rationalize, or ignore what he'd done. But neither did he conclude that because of his mistake God would not or could not use him. The king went on to effective service for God.

Have you owned up to your sin? Fine. Can you move on to meaningful service to God?

That's the question.

29
Daily Bible Reading: Psalms 82-85; Proverbs 18:1-18

Listen and Understand

Devotional Text: Proverbs 18:2

Communication is key. It's key to any relationship.

Communication is also hard. It seems the hardest part is the hearing. We are quick to speak our part, say what we want to say, but don't put much effort into listening. It's like we think the time while the other person is speaking is best spent formulating what we want to say next.

There is a proverb that fits this: "A fool takes no pleasure in understanding, but only in expressing his opinion" (Prov. 18:2).

Do we really think the other person's greatest joy is to hear what we have to say (instead it's probably our greatest joy to hear ourselves talk) or that we will draw the other person over to our way of thinking by the sheer brilliance of our ideas?

The reality is that the influence we can have on another person and for them to even care about what we think is for us to convince them that we are interested in hearing and understanding what they have to say.

Only when they know we care will they begin to listen, and only by genuinely working to understand them will they ever know we care.

30

Daily Bible Reading: 2 Chronicles 22-24; Mark 14:27-52

Jesus' Devotion

Devotional Text: Mark 14:33-34

The familiar words of this hymn are chilling:
Night with ebon pinion, brooded o'er the vale;
All around was silent, save the night wind's wail;
When Christ the man of sorrows, in tears and sweat and blood;
Prostrate in the garden, raised His voice to God.

Mark says of Jesus in Gethsemane that He "began to be very distressed and troubled" and that He confessed to three disciples in the garden, "My soul is deeply grieved to the point of death" (Mark 14:33-34; NASB).

The depth of Jesus' distress matched the magnitude of what He was being asked to do.

No matter what we may have faced or endured or suffered in this life, it just cannot compare to Jesus' garden experience. To become sin in humanity's place on the cross is beyond comprehension and comparison (2 Cor. 5:21).

No wonder the repeated request of God's own Son was to avoid this "cup" and this "hour."

Though Jesus' grief equaled the task at hand, His devotion to the Father's will far exceeded His personal desire for relief from His distress.

Every consideration of Jesus' life leads us ever deeper and deeper into that love which "surpasses knowledge" (Eph. 3:19).

July 31
Daily Bible Reading: 2 Chronicles 25-26; Mark 14:53-72

Good Influences

Devotional Text: 2 Chronicles 26:5

Thank God for good influences. But influences have limitations. At some point a person must take full possession of that good for which they are being influenced.

Think about Uzziah. The king "continued to seek God in the days of Zechariah who had understanding through the vision of God" (2 Chron. 26:5). It appears that as long as Zechariah was around, Uzziah did good. Was it the absence of Zechariah's good influence that allowed for Uzziah's unfaithfulness (2 Chron. 26:16)?

I have known people who, not unlike Uzziah, lost a positive influence in their life, and things seemed to go downhill from there.

Why do I do the right things that I do? Why do I attend Bible study and worship? Why do I serve and help? Is it because of someone else's good influence in my life? That's not a bad thing, but have I taken personal possession and responsibility for the good?

I want as many Zechariahs in my life as I can get. Even more, I want to become what my Zechariahs encourage me to be.

AUGUST

1

Daily Bible Reading: 2 Chronicles 27-29; Mark 15:1-41

Words Fail

Devotional Text: Mark 15:17-20

This is always hard to take:

> *And they clothed him in a purple cloak, and twisting together a crown of thorns, they put it on him. And they began to salute him, "Hail, King of the Jews!" And they were striking his head with a reed and spitting on him and kneeling down in homage to him And when they had mocked him, they stripped him of the purple cloak and put his own clothes on him. And they led him out to crucify him* (Mark 15:17-20).

It was wrong, it was cruel, it was spiteful, indignant, hateful, undeserved, malicious...words fail to adequately describe this heinous act. Jesus was the only perfectly sinless person to ever live. He embodied innocence. He was God, in the flesh, standing there taking this venomous act; no objections, no defense, no response.

> *He was oppressed, and he was afflicted. yet he opened not his mouth; like a lamb that is led to the slaughter, and like a sheep that before its shearers is silent, so he opened not his mouth* (Isaiah 53:7).

I want to scream! The injustice is unbearable and the love is unmistakable.

It is for me. It is for my sin. Jesus received what I deserve and did not say a word.

Again, words fail in the presence of the incomprehensible love of God.

228

2

Daily Bible Reading: 2 Chronicles 30-32; Mark 15:42-16:20

Invading Armies

Devotional Text: 2 Chronicles 32:1

Tell me again why we think that God owes us good things, especially if we're trying to serve Him? Don't tell me people don't think this way. When things don't go the way we want we tend to get upset with God. We even get angry and blame Him. It's not that it's hard to understand why people do this, but at the same time the Bible doesn't support this kind of thinking.

The Bible says things like, "After these things and these acts of faithfulness, Sennacherib king of Assyria came and invaded Judah and encamped against the fortified cities" (2 Chron. 32:1).

What were these "things" and "acts of faithfulness"? "Hezekiah...did what was good and right and faithful before the Lord his God. And every work that he undertook...seeking his God, he did with all his heart, and prospered" (31:20-21).

Still, the invading armies of Sennacherib came. So, the good and right and faithful things in our lives do not guarantee protection from the invasion of hardship, trials, struggles and pain.

So what's the point? This life and this world are not the ultimate goal, they are not what our existence is all about. Remember, "This world is not my home" and "we look not to the things that are seen but to the things that are unseen" (2 Cor. 4:18). My home, my real home, has none of the things that are so painful and distasteful in this life.

In this life God has allowed for sin and unrighteousness and evil. In the life to come they will be dealt with finally, fully, and completely.

3

Daily Bible Reading: 2 Chronicles 33-34; 1 Corinthians 1:1-17

Don't Abandon the Ideal

Devotional Text: 1 Corinthians 1:2

That the church in Corinth had problems, many problems, there can be no doubt.

That Paul considered this group of troubled Christians, Christians, is equally beyond doubt. He addressed them as "the church of God," he believed them to be "sanctified in Christ Jesus," and he referred to them as "saints" (1:2).

His approach from this point forward is remarkable. He did not encourage these various groups and individuals to celebrate their differences. Had he, the end result would have been, well, very much like our present religious climate within Christianity (in the broad sense).

Instead, he said, "I appeal to you, brothers, by the name of our Lord Jesus Christ, that all of you agree, and that there be no divisions among you, but that you be united in the same mind and the same judgment" (1 Cor. 1:10).

No one said this would be easy.

Today's preferred path of justifying the differences within Christianity and pass them off as inevitable or even starts us down a path moving away from, not toward, the apostles' instruction. If we abandon the ideal, what else have we given up on?

4

Daily Bible Reading: 2 Chronicles 35-36; 1 Corinthians 1:18-2:16

Begin Again

Devotional Text: 2 Chronicles 35:16-19

Josiah was a good king, an outstanding king actually (see 2 Chron. 34:2).

He led the people to celebrate the Passover, which had been neglected for some time (35:16-19). This is not unlike his great-grandfather Hezekiah, another outstanding king (see 2 Chron. 31:20-21). He also led in restoring observance of the Passover (see 2 Chron. 30:23-26).

So, two of the most outstanding men to lead God's people were such, in part, because they led the people to return to something that had been, for whatever reason, forsaken.

Maybe the best thing we could do for ourselves right now is to return to something we have been neglecting. It could be any number of things: worship, Bible reading, Bible study, prayer, Christian fellowship, service. The list could go on and on.

What can you do today, something to begin again, that you have not done for some time?

Something you know you should do; something you know God wants you to do?

5

Daily Bible Reading: Psalms 86-88; Proverbs 18:19-19:12

Pure

Devotional Text: Psalm 86:11

Did your parents ever use vocabulary or make statements that still seem odd or curious?

Well, of course. Isn't that part of the definition of being a parent?

One my mom used was "Pure D-O dirt." I have absolutely no idea what the "D-O" thing means, and "pure" dirt seemed contradictory to me for a long time. But it's not.

Something is pure when there is nothing else mixed in with it. Pure gold has all the impurities (there's that word) removed. But you could also have pure nonsense, pure agony, and, yes, pure dirt.

The Bible calls us to be pure, saying, "purify your hearts, you double-minded" (James 4:8). Earlier, James had warned that the trouble with being double-minded is that it leaves one unstable and unfulfilled. How true. A Russian proverb says, "One who chases two hares, catches none."

Single-minded devotion to God is what we're after and the only thing that God will accept. Remember, "But seek first the kingdom of God and his righteousness..." (Matt. 6:33).

So Psalm 86:11 is on this same wavelength with its appeal: "unite my heart to fear your name."

6

Daily Bible Reading: Ezra 1-2; 1 Corinthians 3

God's Crop

Devotional Text: 1 Corinthians 3:9

Not being a farmer, there is much I do not know about that industry. But living in farm country where numerous crops are raised on thousands of acres, some things are pretty clear.

There is a certain beauty to large fields filled with healthy, robust plants without a weed anywhere, but a field of dried-up plants overrun with weeds is an unpleasant and distasteful sight.

We are, the Bible says, God's "field" (1 Cor. 3:9). If God's the farmer, then there is no question what the crops ought to look like.

That's why Paul was disturbed when he looked at the Corinthian Christians and saw "jealousy and strife" among them (1 Cor. 3:3). They weren't strong and mature but weak and stunted, scraggly plants plagued with weeds (1 Cor. 3:14).

Here's the same picture from Hebrews: "For land that has drunk the rain that often falls on it, and produces a crop useful to those for whose sake it is cultivated, receives a blessing from God. But if it bears thorns and thistles, it is worthless and near to being cursed, and its end is to be burned" (Hebrews 6:7-8).

I am God's field. But what does the "crop" look like? With God as the farmer, is it as it should be?

7

Daily Bible Reading: Ezra 3-5; 1 Corinthians 4

Starting Over

Devotional Text: Ezra 5:1

Starting over again; it's not easy, and we would have preferred to have gotten it right the first time, but sometimes there is no other alternative but to begin again.

That's all that was left for God's people. They'd been taken into, first Assyrian, then Babylonian captivity. Their homeland had been ravaged. Now they returned, or at least some of them had. And they began to build again. But where does one begin?

The first group to return from the captivity came to Jerusalem to "rebuild the house of the Lord" (Ezra 1:5). Yet Jerusalem had no walls. No protection was afforded them, and they were terrified (Ezra 3:3).

So, first things first. That wasn't to construct makeshift defenses or to organize a fighting force. Rather, "they built the altar of the God of Israel, as it is written in the Law of Moses the man of God...and they offered burnt offerings on it to the Lord, burnt offerings morning and evening" (Ezra 3:3-4).

When we must begin again the place to start is with God. Uncertainty and instability may feel overwhelming and frightening, so start with what matters the most. Reconnect with your maker and your creator. Reaffirm and reestablish that relationship. Only then will we be ready to tackle the more obvious and visible concerns and threats.

The city of Jerusalem and God's people would make their comeback. Their success and ours all depends on starting in the right place; restore and reaffirm the relationship with God.

8

Daily Bible Reading: Ezra 6-7; 1 Corinthians 5

Christianity's Warts

Devotional Text: 1 Corinthians 5:1

Isn't it irritating when professing Christians live no better lives than unbelievers?

So much so that many people have been "turned off" by Christianity. It's one of the reasons the charge has been filed against Christians and the church that they're nothing but hypocrites.

Though sad and unfortunate, it's actually to be expected. Why? Because it has always been a problem in the church. The Bible's presentation of the church shows us not only its glory as God's people, God's family, and God's possession, but it also shows us the warts that come with the imperfect humans who comprise God's ideal.

At Corinth, immorality existed in the church there "that is not tolerated even among pagans" (1 Cor. 5:1). Does it make sense to reject the church for not being what the Bible never claimed it would be, that is, a body of perfect people? Seriously. For there to be no hypocrites would require perfection. I've met none who made that claim, and if they did, their hypocrisy would be blatantly obvious.

Sin in the church at Corinth in no way rationalizes its presence in our own lives. Paul spoke at length and strongly to rectify that situation (see 1 Cor. 5:1-13).

The truth is, it happens. And to reject God and his plan because it exists, becomes a form of self-condemnation. Putting our own conditions and stipulations on God is unwise to say the least.

9

Daily Bible Reading: Ezra 8-9; 1 Corinthians 6

Act in Faith

Devotional Text: Ezra 8:22-23

A group of Christians decided to take action against the drought that had plagued their region. They decided to act in faith and pray for rain. One young man astutely questioned the faith of the assembled group; not one had brought an umbrella.

Ezra acted in faith as he led the second group of Jews returning from captivity to Jerusalem. He did not request for soldiers to travel with the group to provide protection from enemies because he had told the king, "The hand of our God is for good on all who seek him, and the power of his wrath is against all who forsake him." So, instead, the people fasted and prayed to God "and He listened to [their] entreaty" (Ezra 8:22-23).

It only makes sense that our actions match our professed faith in God.

10

Daily Bible Reading: Ezra 10; Nehemiah 1; 1 Corinthians 7

Marriage is Hard

Devotional Text: 1 Corinthians 7:25

Marriage can be difficult. Many marriages don't succeed. Yet, many still do.

Know that not only is the Bible pro-marriage, it also acknowledges that it can be hard.

1 Corinthians 7 is the great marriage chapter of the Bible (just like 1 Corinthians 13 is the love chapter and Hebrews 11 the faith chapter). It's not nearly as celebrated as the others, and maybe that's because its message is not always easy or preferred.

There are some things in this letter that are challenging and even disputable. Who exactly are the "virgins" spoken of in v. 25 and following? Is it a father's virgin daughter or is it the virgin to which one is committed to be married? And how is it that the "unbelieving" spouse is sanctified or made holy (v. 14)? How is the instruction that each is to remain in the condition which he was called (vv. 17-24) to be applied?

Be sure of this: these may be challenging, but that does not make them unknowable and therefore not applicable to us. And further, given the types of instruction provided here by Paul, marriage is hard work. Without doubt, a successful marriage demands two people committed to go the extra mile, sacrifice, and submit themselves to their spouse for the good of the relationship.

Remember, marriage is not a social invention of man, rather it is a divinely provided means by which God has cared for our greatest needs and blessed us with our greatest potential blessings.

11
Daily Bible Reading: Nehemiah 2-3; 1 Corinthians 8

Good Leadership

Devotional Text: Nehemiah 2:5

Surely one of the greatest examples of leadership in all the Bible is Nehemiah. This man led the third great return of the Israelites back to Jerusalem from captivity to rebuild the walls of Jerusalem.

Note the following about this man and what he did:

• He was not in a position of leadership to do what he did. He was a cupbearer for the king of Persia. Nothing about that "qualified" him to lead the returning Jews or rebuild a wall.

• He learned about a need and moved to fulfill it. Word about the deplorable condition of the walls of Jerusalem and the city itself was all it took for him to be moved to action. No one asked him to do it, no one told him he should.

• He took responsibility. How long had the city and walls been in this condition? How much longer would they have remained like this had he not done something about it? No one knows. But Nehemiah stepped up and did what needed to be done.

• He assessed the situation and developed his plan. Nehemiah's famous nighttime ride gave him valuable firsthand information about the circumstances. He was not going to going to jump into the situation without a plan of action.

Many more valuable lessons are there to be learned from Nehemiah. But we have to quit thinking about leadership in terms of "position" and that responsibility lies solely with such people. Rather, don't wait for someone to tell you. What needs to be done? Gather the information you need and develop a plan of attack.

12

Daily Bible Reading: Psalm 89; Proverbs 19:13-29

Serene Wisdom

Devotional Text: Proverbs 19:13-29

The so-called "Serenity Prayer" is well known. It talks about changing the things we can and accepting the things we can't and having the wisdom to know the difference.

Proverbs helps provide that wisdom as it regularly identifies things that are troublesome and problematic in life and encourages us to take action that leads to a better life.

Note the following areas of potential difficulties from the small sampling of reading in Proverbs today:
> family relationships
> laziness and idleness
> careless actions
> anger
> lying and dishonesty

Also note what can be done with positive effect:
> keep God's commandments
> show generosity to the poor
> discipline children
> hear wise counsel
> be faithful and loyal
> fear the Lord
> accept reproof

How much more serene would our lives be simply following Proverbs' wisdom?

13
Daily Bible Reading: Nehemiah 4-6; 1 Corinthians 9

Do It All

Devotional Text: 1 Corinthians 9:23

How much do I want salvation? How strong does my desire for heaven burn?

Paul had an interesting way to express this. He said, "I do it all for the sake of the gospel, that I may share with them in its blessing" (1 Cor. 9:23). The question is, what is the "all" that Paul was willing to do to share in the gospel's blessing?

We might initially think of the persecutions and hardship he endured (see 2 Cor. 11:23-28). That is itself rather astounding. But even more impressive is the willingness of Paul to forego his own personal rights for the sake of reaching others with Jesus' message. He went to great lengths to insure that people with whom he worked had the best opportunity to hear and embrace the gospel. He went so far as to say that, "though I am free from all men, I have made myself a slave to all, that I might win more of them" (1 Cor. 9:19; NASB). Paul voluntarily put himself in servitude to others for the gospel's sake.

How strong is my own desire to share in the gospel's blessings? Its greatest measure is not found in how much I am willing to endure, but rather in how far I'm willing to go in sacrificing my own rights that others might have the opportunity to know Jesus Christ.

14

Daily Bible Reading: Nehemiah 7; 1 Corinthians 10:1-11:1

Godliness in Leadership

Devotional Text: Nehemiah 7:2

What makes a man qualified to lead or to be placed in a position of responsibility?

Of course, qualifications for the required tasks do come into play. But if that's the final measure, we've fallen short in selecting our leaders. There is so much more to it than we often think.

After Nehemiah had rebuilt Jerusalem's walls, he sought out a man to be in "charge over Jerusalem" (Neh. 7:2). So, what kind of man would that be? Would he seek out the best administrator? A motivator of men? Or perhaps the greatest decisionmaker?

The fact is, while any of these might have been true, the only thing that is said of the one given this great responsibility is that he was "a more faithful and God-fearing man than many" (Neh. 7:2).

Being a spiritual, godly man does not necessarily make a person a good leader, but a leader will never be his best apart from godliness.

15
Daily Bible Reading: Nehemiah 8-9; 1 Corinthians 11:2-34

One Thing: Good or Bad

Devotional Text: 1 Corinthians 11:2, 17

No one is all good, neither is anyone all bad. Good can be found in the worst, and bad can be found in the best. It's true of people, and it's true of bodies of the Lord's church. Paul told the Christians, in 1 Corinthians 11, both, "I commend you" and "I do not commend you" (vv. 2, 17). They had done some things well and some things they had not.

The important thing here is what happens next. Either situation can turn out for the good or for the bad. Here's what I mean. Take a person who has done one thing well. They sometimes "camp" on that thing and act as if that is all there is. Any attempt to point out some failing or fault in another area is met with a reminder of the one thing done well.

They act as if that one commendable thing defines their entire being. On the other hand, when someone has failed in one particular area, they can easily come to think as though that defines them. That one area of failing means, in their mind, that they are a complete and total failure.

The good in us serves as a starting point. We begin from there and build and improve in other areas as well. We gain confidence from the good we've done but honestly realize we can do better.

The bad in us needs corrected. All of us fail and fall short of God's ideal. That's part of being human. It only defines us when we don't find a solution and work to fix that failing.

The issue, then, is not whether or not you have something commendable about you, but rather what you will do with it, good or bad, from here.

242

16
Daily Bible Reading: Nehemiah 10-11; 1 Corinthians 12

God's House

Devotional Text: Nehemiah 10:39

During Nehemiah's day the people of God made a noble commitment: they would not be neglectful of God's house (Neh. 10:39).

How they intended to carry out this commitment is explained in chapter 10. It involved consecrating themselves to God and His service, providing financial support, making a schedule of ones to provide wood to the priests for use on the altar, bringing the firstfruits of the crops and the firstborn of their livestock, giving tithes of their produce for use by the priests and Levites, and so on.

To neglect God's house would be a great shame.

God has a house yet today. Despite the terminology used by many, it's not the church building or place of the church's assembly. God's house is His people. It is His family, the church: "...but Christ is faithful over God's house as a son. And we are his house if indeed we hold fast our confidence and our boasting in our hope" (Heb. 3:6).

Will we commit ourselves that God's house not be neglected? How so? By regular and faithful attendance to it's assemblies, by encouraging and supporting its leadership, by devoting ourselves to the church's work, by giving generously, by visiting and calling on fellow Christians in time of need, and on it goes.

God's house demands our attention.

17
Daily Bible Reading: Nehemiah 12-13; 1 Corinthians 13

Amazing Love

Devotional Text: 1 Corinthians 13

Love is amazing.

That's not the most profound, eloquent, or moving thing ever written about love. But it is true.

What does fit into the category of "The Best Things Ever Written About Love" is 1 Corinthians 13.

The absence of love makes otherwise remarkable acts and abilities worthless (vv. 13).

Love's description in terms of actions done and not done (vv. 4-7) reminds me of how often I fail at love. Love is better, much better, than miracles (vv. 8-12). Love outlasts everything, even some of the best things God has given us, like faith and hope (v. 13).

Here's the kicker. 1 Corinthians 13 wasn't written for husbands and wives (though it does apply and has made its appearance in innumerable weddings). It wasn't written for warring nations (applies here too) or as a business leadership manifesto (a couple of recent books apply it this way).

1 Corinthians 13 was written to teach Christians how they should treat each other, and everybody else while we're at it (Luke 6:27).

Love isn't reserved only for the closest, most precious, and intimate relationships; it is for every relationship.

18
Daily Bible Reading: Esther 1-3; 1 Corinthians 14

Do What Esther Did

Devotional Text: Esther 2:7

Don't hate Esther.

She embodied the very things that prompt many people to dislike others. Esther was beautiful, charming, and apparently possessed quite a winsome personality. Everyone loved her, and that's why people might hate her. Esther was everything that so many of us are not.

Without doubt, God used Esther to accomplish His will. What is more, it was those very traits on which God's providence capitalized to put Esther in the place where she could become an instrument of God's will.

Do not miss the point here. It is not that if you are not beautiful and charming and win, some that you are worthless, that's culture's message, not God's. Rather it is that God can use who you are to His glory, if you'll let Him. It is not to that we need to be pretty like Esther, but that we must put ourselves out there where we can become useful to God.

Esther was pretty before God used her. Afterward she was indescribably beautiful, and it had nothing to do with how she looked.

19

Daily Bible Reading: Psalm 90-92; Proverbs 20:1-18

My Little For God's Great Glory

Devotional Text: Psalm 90:1

Get over yourself. Really.

One of the very best things we can do for ourselves is to get over ourselves.

I know that we are trained and cajoled and bombarded with messages that bring us to think our existence transpires in the "universe of me." It does not.

God, not me, is the framework of our existence. He comes before everything that has come before us (Ps. 90:1).

The very best humanity has ever offered is now dust (v. 3), as will be my very best. All great people, nations, or civilizations are swept away as a flood and have no more substance now than a dream (v. 5). Can I expect any more for myself?

At best, the time of our life will span some seventy years, maybe eighty if we are strong (v. 10). We are really not even around long enough to matter much; especially compared to God for whom 1,000 years is no more significant than yesterday, or a watch in the night, when it's gone (v. 4).

"So teach us to number our days that we may get a heart of wisdom" (v. 12).

I really do need to get over myself and plan to use my few days to God's glory.

20

Daily Bible Reading: Esther 4-7; 1 Corinthians 15:1-34

A Mountainous Text

Devotional Text: 1 Corinthians 15:3

This text is epic. I mean, really.

Some people view the Bible as a flat landscape with all parts and portions being equally important. I suppose there's a sense in which that is true. The Bible is also a rich and varied topography. Some passages soar in meaning and significance and importance.

1 Corinthians 15 is like the Himalayas. This is heady stuff. It's really big. Paul talks about matters of "first importance" (v. 3). He says that if these thingsthe resurrection of Jesusaren't true, then faith itself is worthless (v. 14), our very salvation is empty (17), and Christians are the most pitiful people in the world (v. 19).

But they are true. Jesus did raise from the dead. And that changes everything!

21
Daily Bible Reading: Esther 8-10; 1Corinthians 15:35-58

Almighty God and Me

Devotional Text: Esther 8:12

"My God is big, so strong and so mighty, there's nothing my God cannot do."

So the words of a children's song go, accompanied by the appropriate hand motions, of course. That's an important message to get across to little ones and one needed by more than just a few older ones too.

Has our understanding of God's power and might matured along with our bodies, minds, and faith? The limitless power of God as fully displayed in Scripture contributes greatly to our faith. But as the end of the book of Esther shows, that does not mean there is no place for me in the equation.

Wicked Haman, thanks to God's providential working, was out of the picture. Still, the efforts he set in motion were still at work. God's people were still threatened throughout the Persian Empire. Esther and Mordecai still had work to do. And they did it.

God's might is not necessarily exercised by His doing everything. Sometimes it is by providing us the opportunity to get done what needs done.

True, there is nothing my God cannot do. What He sometimes does, though, is give me the opportunity to act.

22

Daily Bible Reading: Job 1-3; 1 Corinthians 16

Opportunities and Adversaries

Devotional Text: 1 Corinthians 16:9

I like a good opportunity. So did Paul.

He described his as "a wide door for effective work" in Ephesus (1 Cor. 16:9). He doesn't elaborate on the nature of that opportunity other than to add, "and there are many adversaries."

What?

Would my mind allow me to think of adversaries and opportunities in the same context?

Or would the presence of adversariesor any other troubleby definition prevent me from considering the situation to be an opportunity? Adversaries mean a problem, not an opportunity, right?

Perhaps we need to rethink this. The presence of adversaries, means that not only is everyone not in agreement with what we're doing, but some are in opposition. Are we of a mind to think consensus is a necessary requirement to move forward? It will never happen. What is more, we may rest assured that if we are going to push forward, there will be no lack of people who push back. And don't be surprised when among them are ones you expected to be pushing with you, not against.

It doesn't matter if we're talking about personal endeavors or those we make as a family, a church family, for the cause of righteousness, or whatever, we must become accustomed to the idea that when opportunities show up, adversaries are part of the package.

23
Daily Bible Reading: Job 4-6, 2 Corinthians 1:1-2:11

Would I Still Trust?

Devotional Text: Job 6:23

Job suffered much. Understandably, he struggled with it.

He suggested that if all his vexation and calamities were placed in a balance, their weight would equal the sands of the sea (Job 6:23). The implication was that his suffering far outweighed any wrongdoing on his part.

In other words, "This is not fair!"

Trying to understand the hardships and difficulties of life in terms of what is fair is a fruitless effort.

Job's experience was not about his receiving what he deserved, though his "friends" attempted to interpret it that way. Rather, it was about the genuineness and depth of Job's faith and trust in God.

His relationship with God was not based on the fact that God had been good to him (as Satan contended). The only way to prove this was for the good things to be removed and see what happened.

Yes, Job struggled and even complained, but never lost his confidence in God.

Is my own relationship with God based only on His goodness to me? What if the good is removed? Will I still trust in him?

24

Daily Bible Reading: Job 7-9; 2 Corinthians 2:12-3:18

Do You Smell Something?

Devotional Text: 2 Corinthians 2:14-15

American culture is very picky about smell. Nothing turns us off quite like an unpleasant odor. That's especially true when it originates from a person. We know what "B-O" stands for, and we don't like it. Just travel to some other culture, and it really doesn't matter which, and one of the most striking differences will have to do with how people smell. It's true.

Paul used a rather unusual idea to describe God's people when he addressed their odor.

Through us, he says, God "spreads the fragrance of the knowledge of him everywhere. For we are the aroma of Christ to God among those who are being saved and those who are perishing" (2 Cor. 2:14-15).

I have to ask myself if that is truly an apt description of me. By my manner of living, my attitudes, my conduct, my interaction with others, my demeanor, my speech, my influence, can I really be called "the aroma of Christ"?

What do people "smell" when they're around me?

25

Daily Bible Reading: Job 10-12; 2 Corinthians 4:1-5:10

Life Can Hurt

Devotional Text: Job 10:23

Sometimes it is hard to understand. It just is.

Job didn't understand. He didn't understand why such suffering and hardship had come into his own life. Why was God punishing him like this? What made it worse was it appeared that God was ignoring the wrongs of the wicked.

"I will say to God, 'Do not condemn me; let me know why you contend against me.

Does it seem good to you to oppress, to despise the work of your hands and favor the designs of the wicked?'" (Job 10:23). What Job did not yet understand, but as readers of Job's story we do, His suffering was not God's punishment. Rather, it was the work of Satan, which God allowed. The whole point was to prove Job did not serve God only when blessed and protected by Him, but even in midst of adversity.

Still, it was a hard pill to swallow. Job gave "full vent to [his] complaint" and spoke "in the bitterness of [his] soul" (Job 10:1; NASB). He was hurting.

Our own hardships and struggles do not mean God is displeased. Perhaps this is the refining fire that will purify and strengthen our faith (1 Pet. 1:7) or the discipline of the Lord that He brings on those whom He loves so that our lives might produce the "peaceful fruit of righteousness" (Heb. 12:7-11).

26
Daily Bible Reading: Psalms 93-96; Proverbs 20:19-21:6

More Important Than Worship

Devotional Text: Proverbs 21:3

Some things are just more important to God than others. It's remarkable how often we get those things confused, though. We act as though God's greatest desire of us is to be religious, worshiping people. As though that were an end in itself.

Yet, how often is the message of Scripture to the contrary.
- "To do righteousness and justice is more acceptable to the Lord than sacrifice" (Prov. 21:3).
- "Has the LORD as great delight in burnt offerings and sacrifices, as in obeying the voice of the LORD? Behold, to obey is better than sacrifice, and to listen than the fat of rams" (1 Sam. 15:22).
- "For I desire steadfast love and not sacrifice, the knowledge of God rather than burnt offerings" (Hosea 6:6).
- "Will the LORD be pleased with thousands of rams, with ten thousands of rivers of oil? Shall I give my firstborn for my transgression, the fruit of my body for the sin of my soul? He has told you, O man, what is good; and what does the LORD require of you but to do justice, and to love kindness, and to walk humbly with your God?" (Micah 6:7-8).
- "Go and learn what this means, 'I desire mercy, and not sacrifice'" (Matt. 9:13).

The fact is we can be religious and be very far from what God wants and expects of us. Primarily, He wants us to be righteous, just, obedient, and kind. He wants us to know Him, walk humbly with Him and to have steadfast love. If those things are as they should be, the worship and religion will take care of itself.

27

Daily Bible Reading: Job 13-14; 2 Corinthians 5:11-6:13

Lots of People

Devotional Text: 2 Corinthians 5:19

People, like water in James Casey's poem, are everywhere. Humans provide endless variation. That's true not only in shapes and size and appearance but in personality as well. Some are beautiful; some are not. Some are pleasant; some are not. Some are likeable; some are not.

What do I think of them? What are they to me?

They are at the same time all different, and all the same.

They are all the same in that they are all loved by Christ. He therefore died for them that they might all be reconciled to God, that is their trespasses, which all have, would not be held against them (2 Cor. 5:19).

It is that same love of Christ that should control us, including how we think about people (2 Cor. 5:14). We, like Paul, should be moved to persuade men, all men (v. 11); persuade them to be reconciled to God (v. 20).

For all the variety in the human race there is really only one difference in people that matters, that is whether or not they have been reconciled to God. If they have, they are "in Christ" and a "new creation" (v. 17). If they have, they "no longer live for themselves but for him who for their sake died and was raised" (v. 15).

People, people everywhere; people needing reconciliation to God.

28

Daily Bible Reading: Job 15-16; 2 Corinthians 6:14-7:16

The Right Kind of Comforter

Devotional Text: Job 16:2

People hurt. The Bible says that life is characterized by two things, brevity and troubles (Job 14:1).

Job, of course, had his fair share of those troubles. The friends who came to him did not make things any better. Job said of them, "miserable comforters are you all" (Job. 16:2). They were attempting to explain why these bad things were happening to him. That was no help at all.

For one thing, they were wrong. They tried to tell Job it was punishment for some great sin he had committed, but Job knew that was not the case. Explanations and theological reasoning are of no value to one who is suffering. Knowing that someone else may be suffering more or that one has other things for which to be thankful, or being provided with a rationale for what has taken place does nothing to alleviate the pain one is enduring; nothing.

Paul says the only time we're really equipped to provide comfort is when we have been comforted by God ourselves in our affliction (2 Cor. 1:3-4). That means we have been there and we have experienced the pain. Therefore we know how hollow and empty many well-meaning words can be. Instead, we are there with a warm embrace and a sympathetic ear. No explanations, no reasons for why they should not feel as they do, no comparisons with somebody else's suffering.

Miserable comforters just add to the misery. Genuine comforters give support and space to experience and process the pain. It's the only way it works.

29

Daily Bible Reading: Job 17-19; 2 Corinthians 8-9

Life Aligned With God

Devotional Text: 2 Corinthians 9:8

In one place Paul talks about the power of God working in the Christian "far more abundantly than all that we ask or think" (Eph. 3:20). Wow.

Here's another one: "And God is able to make all grace abound to you, so that having all sufficiency in all things at all times, you may abound in every good work" (2 Cor. 9:8). It's just hard to grasp all that we're being told here. And I use the word "all" advisedly. Notice how many times it shows up in English in this verse, four times. A form of the same word is also translated "every" as well.

Is there ever a time or a place or a circumstance or a need for which God has not provided completely for everything? Why, then do we sometimes feel inadequate or ill-equipped or insufficient? Perhaps it's because of what we're trying to accomplish. Notice that God does this so we might "abound in every good work."

When our lives and efforts are aligned with God's purposes, zealously doing the good works for which He has created us (see Eph. 2:10 and Titus 2:14), then we lack nothing.

It's only when life is out of kilter with God that we are suddenly in a state of want.

So, what God provides is directly related to the alignment of my life with God's purpose.

It's always a good time to evaluate, assess, and realign.

30

Daily Bible Reading: Job 20-21; 2 Corinthians 10:1-11:15

Do I Have it Right?

Devotional Text: Job 20:27-29

Job's friends were convinced his misfortune was due to his own sin.

Zophar says it again: "The heavens will reveal his iniquity, and the earth will rise up against him. The possessions of his house will be carried away, dragged off in the day of God's wrath. This is the wicked man's portion from God, the heritage decreed for him by God" (Job 20:27-29).

Job knew it could not be true. One reason was that if that's the way it worked, then neither would any good thing ever come to any wicked man. But it does. "Why do the wicked live, reach old age, and grow mighty in power?" (Job 21:7). What is more, in their prosperity they ask, "What is the Almighty that we should serve him? And what profit do we get if we pray to him?" (Job 21:15).

Though Job has no good answer as to why the wicked prosper, he did know that the fact they can and do is evidence that his own suffering was not due to wrong he had done.

God's ways are not our ways, and His thoughts are not our own (Isa. 55:8). Among other things, that means how He works in this world will often be beyond our comprehension.

Let's not be too quick to think we've got it all figured out.

31
Daily Bible Reading: Job 22-24; 2 Corinthians 11:16-12:10

Wants vs. Needs

Devotional Text: 2 Corinthians 12:7

Do I want it, or do I need it? That can get a little fuzzy.

If we're thinking about physical things, yes we can probably agree that genuine needs are few. Beyond that, though, we may not be able to make the distinction at all.

I think Paul struggled with this. He had his unidentified "thorn in the flesh" (2 Cor. 12:7). Efforts to identify the thorn are not only guesswork, they are pointless. It doesn't matter what it was. We only know it was a "messenger of Satan" and it harassed Paul.

Paul was convinced that his need in this situation was the removal of the thorn. To that end he prayed three times for its removal. God's determination was the thorn's presence served an important purpose for Paul. What he needed was not that it should leave him, but that he rely even more on God's sufficient grace (v. 9).

Am I convinced of what I need from God? Maybe I know and maybe I don't. Maybe it's just a want and He'll give me what I really need, whether I know it or not or want it or not.

SEPTEMBER

1
Daily Bible Reading: Job 25-28; 2 Corinthians 12:11-13:14

Acquiring Understanding

Devotional Text: Job 28:1-11

We know how to find what we want, don't we? After all, can't we enter just one or two keywords in our favorite search engine (i.e., Google, Bing, Yahoo) and be instantaneously (provided it's not a dialup connection) presented with a multitude of possible sources for what we want?

Job knew nothing of the internet, but he did know about finding what we want. In his day, one had to work a bit harder to get it. Still, he says that man knows how to acquire what is important and valuable to him and he will go to great lengths to do so.

He describes mines and the mining process to find silver, gold, copper, iron and precious gems (Job 28:1-11).

Yes, but what about wisdom and understanding? Where is it found? There are a number of problems in regards to it. First of all, man does not understand or appreciate its value, which is much greater than everything else he works so hard to get. What is more, nothing of value can be given in exchange to get it (vv. 13-19).

Second, not realizing its value, man does not pursue it as he ought. Not compared to his efforts to acquire precious metals and gems.

And third, there is only one place for it to be found, and that is with God. It won't come into our possession by our hard work and ingenuity nor by an exchange for our trinkets and baubles. Only by fearing God and turning from evil can it be found (v. 28).

Apparently a price too high for most people.

2

Daily Bible Reading: Psalms 97-101; Proverbs 21:7-25

Goals and Objectives

Devotional Text: Psalm 101:2,3,5,6

What are your goals and objectives?

Perhaps it's to be able to retire by a certain age? Or maybe to attain to a certain level of wealth? Could it be a career goal? What about something health related like a target weight or cholesterol or blood pressure level or maybe being able to run a certain distance?

Whatever it is, you know there have to be specific, achievable steps along the way to finally reach it. You don't reach the top of a flight of stairs in one mighty jump; rather, it is literally one step at a time.

What about spiritual goals? What is more, what are the "steps" you are taking to reach them? Consider these from Psalm 101:
- Think about living blamelessly. "I will ponder the way that is blameless" (v. 2). We'll not achieve the ideal, but we should keep it in our minds always.
- Live and act privately as you try to do publicly. "I will walk with integrity in my house" (v. 2).
- Avoid not just what is evil, but also what has no value or worth. "I will not set before my eyes anything that is worthless" (v. 3).
- Be mindful of the daily influences on your life by those with whom you associate. Avoid the one who slanders or is haughty, but "look with favor on the faithful in the land" and "he who walks in the way that is blameless" (vv. 5-6). Surround yourself, as best you can, with those whose goals and intentions match your own.

Heaven is indeed the goal. What am I doing today to help make that goal a reality?

3

Daily Bible Reading: Job 29-30; Hebrews 1:1-2:4

Selling Jesus Short

Devotional Text: Hebrews 1:2-4

Don't sell Jesus short. Most people do.

It is likely more of a challenge than we might think.

It's not unusual to hear complimentary statements regarding Jesus, even from ones who don't believe in Him. Even many believers' ideas regarding the Nazarene fail to reach the height of His reality.

The great book of Hebrews opens with an impressive list of truths about Christ:
- God has spoken to us through Him (v. 2).
- God appointed Him heir of all things (v. 2).
- God created all things through Him (v. 3).
- He radiates God's glory (v. 3).
- He is the exact imprint of God's nature (v. 3).
- He upholds the universe by the word of His power (v. 3).
- He has made purification for our sins (v. 3).
- He is enthroned at God's right hand (v. 3).
- His place is much superior to that of angels (v. 4).

Most of us will have to work to bring our thinking about Jesus up to God's revelation of His beloved Son.

Just do not sell Him short.

4

Daily Bible Reading: Psalms Job 31-32; Hebrews 2:5-3:6

Be Careful Little Eyes

Devotional Text: Job 31:1

I remember singing as a child a song that said, "Oh be careful little eyes what you see..."

I just didn't know at the time I'd need to keep singing that for the rest of my life.

Jesus taught that the eye, and what comes into our minds and lives through it, is key to whether or not our lives are full of light or darkness (Matt. 6:22-23).

Further demonstrating the critical spiritual impact of the eye, He said, "If your right eye causes you to sin, tear it out and throw it away. For it is better that you lose one of your members than that your whole body be thrown into hell" (Matt. 5:29).

So, John also warns that the "desires of the eyes" prompt a love of the world, which cannot coexist with the love of the Father (1 John 2:15-16).

The Psalmist's efforts to live righteously included the resolve to not "set before my eyes anything that is worthless" (Psalm 101:3).

So, Job says, "I have made a covenant with my eyes" (Job 31:1).

Now there's an idea. What agreement, deal, contract, or arrangement will you make with your own eyes so that they do not become your spiritual downfall?

5

Daily Bible Reading: Job 33-34; Hebrews 3:7-4:13

Be Warned

Devotional Text: Hebrews 3:12

I've often wondered if anyone was ever really affected by the Surgeon General's warning that, by law, appears on every packet of cigarettes? Maybe so. Don't you think though it's been seen so many times that it doesn't even register in the buyer's mind anymore?

I wonder if the same thing is true for Christians and the dire warning of Hebrews 3:12, "Take care, brothers, lest there be in any of you an evil, unbelieving heart, leading you to fall away from the living God."

Do we take that seriously or pass it off as really being for some other Christians and not us?

Maybe part of the problem is knowing what is meant by "unbelieving heart." After all we'd say we are far from ceasing to believe in God-very far.

Notice how he goes on to define this type of heart as exemplified by the Israelites in the wilderness (vv. 13-19). They "provoked" God by failing to take the land when it was being given to them (v. 17). They "sinned" by their unfaithfulness and so died in the wilderness (v. 17). They were "disobedient" in not doing as God had told them (v. 18), and thus "unbelief" (v. 19) was true of them though they never came to the point of renouncing belief in God.

Unbelief is not as far from us as we may think.

Be warned.

6

Daily Bible Reading: Job 35-36; Hebrews 4:14-5:10

Learning From My Teacher

Devotional Text: Job 36:22

Who is a teacher like God? (Job 36:22).

Indeed.

God knows all. He reveals what He would have us know. His will is able to be fully known. We have it all in a book free for our consumption and enrichment.

He teaches us about Himself in the created world where we live. His eternal power and divine nature are on constant display (Rom. 1:20). His glory and splendor are being proclaimed through the expanse of heaven (Ps. 8:1; 19:1), His righteousness too (Ps. 50:6; 97:6).

His people serve as encouragement and reinforcement of His instructions for godliness (Ps. 101:6).

There is no teacher like God.

How am I as a student?

7

Daily Bible Reading: Job 37-38; Hebrews 5:11-6:20

Growing or Maturing?

Devotional Text: Hebrews 6:13

I don't enjoy getting older like I used to. As a child, there were few things as thrilling as birthdays, and those milestones just couldn't come fast enough. Every child wants to grow up; it's only natural.

Or do they?

Some Christians, spiritually speaking, never mature past childhood and appear to have no intention of doing so. Perhaps they are oblivious to their condition or just assume their growth will come as naturally and consistently as birthdays.

It doesn't work that way.

By definition, a spiritual child is one "who lives on milk and is unskilled in the word of righteousness" (Heb. 6:13). Now, there is a time when that is completely natural and appropriate. Everyone has to start at the beginning. But no one should remain there.

God's plan for every one of His children is that they "go on to maturity" (Heb. 6:1). That involves progressing from a diet of "milk" to one of the "solid food" of God's Word (Heb. 5:12). That "solid food" is for "those who have their powers of discernment trained by constant practice to distinguish good from evil" (v. 14).

Do not think that spiritual maturity will come as inevitably as your next birthday. Rather, it demands our attentiveness to God's word. Simply put, when we stop listening (Heb. 5:11; "dull of hearing"), we stop growing.

8

Daily Bible Reading: Job 39-40; Hebrews 7

Am I Right, Or is God?

Devotional Text: Job 40:8

Is God to blame?

What for? For anything that doesn't seem to be right in this world or in my life. For my troubles and problems and the sources of anxiety. For times when things don't go my way.

Is He at fault? Or has He at least failed for not protecting me or for not solving my problems? Job thought so. That is until God cross-examined him. "Will you even put me in the wrong? Will you condemn me that you may be in the right?" (Job 40:8).

God made an adjustment to the way Job looked at things. One way was by reminding him of just how ignorant he really was by virtue of the onslaught of questions for which Job had no answer (Job 38-41). Would he, then, presume to suggest that he knew more about even his own circumstances than God?

The other way God adjusted Job's thinking was to show him the reality of what he was doing. He was condemning God so that he would be right. It was all an effort to justify himself. For that to be true, God, then, would have to be wrong.

Really? Are we willing to put God at fault just so we can be right? Rather, as Paul said, "Let God be proven true, and every human being shown up as a liar" (Rom. 3:4; NET).

Job's problem was no different than our problem. Our greatest concern is for making ourselves right, even at God's expense.

9
Daily Bible Reading: Psalms 102-105; Proverbs 21:26-22:12

A Parental Challenge

Devotional Text: Proverbs 22:6

"I never thought about it that way."

Ever had that experience? A different perspective on a familiar idea or thought that opened previously unseen possibilities? It happens far too infrequently. We can get caught in ruts of thinking just as easily as ruts of behavior.

One of the best known and most cited Proverbs of all is, "Train up a child in the way he should go; even when he is old he will not depart from it" (Prov. 22:6). Some translations have an alternative reading here that shines a different light on this text.

"Train up a child according to his way..."

Every parent with more than one child recognizes that no two children are alike.

Sometimes it is shocking how different two kids from the same genetic material and raised in the same environment can be. They have very different ways of thinking and responses to stimuli and talents and interests. It is a fallacy to think every child, even in the same household, can be handled exactly the same.

One of a parent's greatest challenges is learning his or her own child and then rearing that child in terms of who they are, in the way of the Lord.

268

10

Daily Bible Reading: Job 41-42; Hebrews 8

Where Jesus Is

Devotional Text: Hebrews 8:1

Location! Location! Location!

Those are the three most important factors for having a successful busi-ness, or so we're told. Those are also--and more importantly--three of the most important truths to know about Jesus.

What?

The book of Hebrews drives the point home of Jesus' location five times; in today's reading: "...one who is seated at the right hand of the throne of the Majesty in heaven" (Heb. 8:1; see also 1:3, 13; 10:12; 12:2).

Location. Location. Location.

What's the point? Actually there are several.
- Jesus is seated, having completed the task He came to do, that is to make purification for all sins for all time (Heb. 1:3; 10:12).
- Jesus is seated at the right hand of God's throne as He now reigns, with God, over His kingdom (Acts 2:30-35).
- Being at God's right hand, Jesus occupies the loftiest of all positions, rivaled by none else (Heb. 1:13).
- Jesus is in God's presence, serving as my advocate and mediator (1 John 2:1; 1 Tim. 2:5).
- When I approach the throne of grace, Jesus is already there. No wonder we there "receive mercy and find grace to help in time of need" (Heb. 4:16).

Thank God for Jesus' location!

11
Daily Bible Reading: Ecclesiastes 1-3; Hebrews 9

Under the Sun

Devotional Text: Ecclesiastes 1

Life is futile! It is worthless and it is meaningless. Generations come and go, but what comes of it? The sun rises, the sun sets. Nothing ever changes. The wind blows here and it blows there, but what does it accomplish? All of the rivers and streams eventually make it to the sea, but it is never filled up.

What has been, will be. What has been done, will be done again. It's true. It really is...from the perspective "under the sun" (Ecc. 1).

That is exactly how the book of Ecclesiastes begins. If our only perspective is "under the sun" that is, if there is only what we can see and experience in this physical existence then yes, life is absolutely futile. The greatest knowledge, the greatest accomplishments, the greatest pleasure, the greatest folly just doesn't matter.

But that is exactly the point, isn't it? God, who definitely is not "under the sun," changes everything. I and you and everyone and everything else takes on a whole new meaning when God is part of the equation.

Do we understand just how destructive the efforts to eliminate, or at the very least marginalize, God are to humanity? In the name of science and philosophy, out of pride and conceit, in the pursuit of tolerance and equanimity, we refuse to allow God His rightful place. Don't we know we are damning ourselves to worthlessness, meaninglessness, and futility?

We could sure use a little wisdom here, and that is precisely what Ecclesiastes delivers.

12

Daily Bible Reading: Ecclesiastes 4-7; Hebrews 10:1-18

Jesus is Impressive

Devotional Text: Hebrews 10:7

What is most impressive about Jesus to you?

Is it that He willingly left heaven?

Is it that in His absolute purity and innocence He did not respond to those who wished Him dead?

Is it His ability to so deftly and masterfully handle every attack and attempt to trap Him in His words?

Is it His limitless patience with disciples who time after time failed to understand?

There are so many traits and qualities with which to be impressed.

To me, one of the most admirable is that He carried through perfectly where I fail so miserably, so often; "Behold, I have come to do your will, O God" (Heb. 10:7).

13

Daily Bible Reading: Ecclesiastes 8-10; Hebrews 10:19-39

Sharpen Your Axe

Devotional Text: Ecclesiastes 10:10

Abraham Lincoln said that if he were given six hours in which to cut wood, he'd spend the first four sharpening his axe.

So also are the words of "the Preacher" (Ecc. 1:1): "If the iron is blunt, and one does not sharpen the edge, he must use more strength" (Ecc. 10:10).

So what is it that "sharpens our axe" for living life? The verse goes on to say, "Wisdom helps one to succeed." Surely we know that is true. Wisdom is going to help make life easier and better.

So we want to know, like Job, "From where shall wisdom be found?" and "From where, then, does wisdom come?" (Job 28:12, 20). He affirms the fear of the Lord, "that is wisdom" (v. 28).

It is just as Proverbs says, "The fear of the Lord is the beginning of wisdom, and the knowledge of the Holy One is insight" (Prov. 9:10).

There's no way around it. A successful life demands wisdom, and wisdom begins with the fear of the Lord.

Get to sharpening your axe!

14

Daily Bible Reading: Ecclesiastes 11-12;
Song of Solomon 1-2; Hebrews 11:1-22

Soul Preserve

Devotional Text: Hebrews 10:39

Without question, Hebrews 11 is among the most famous Bible chapters: the great "Faith chapter" with all of these great men and women who "by faith" did so much.

We often forget chapter 11's place in the larger message of the book. The writer is working to divert his audience from throwing away their confidence, that they would "live by faith" and not "shrink back" (10:35, 38). One course has great reward, the other God has no pleasure in.

Then comes this charge at the very end of chapter 10: "But we are not of those who shrink back to destruction, but of those who have faith to the preserving of the soul" (Heb 10:39; NASB).

What kind of faith preserves the soul? Chapter 11 is an extended illustration and explanation of exactly that. It's the kind of faith demonstrated by all of these godly ones.

It is faith that does not shrink back because it moves people to action; to offer and walk and construct and obey and to go as did Abel and Enoch and Noah and Abraham and so on.

So is our faith one of two kinds; but which is it?

15
Daily Bible Reading: Song of Solomon 3-6; Hebrews 11:23-40

A Blessed Gift

Devotional Text: Song of Solomon 6:3

God gives many gifts, and they are "good" and "perfect" (James 1:17).

The unique book of the Song of Solomon, or Song of Songs, celebrates what is most certainly one of those gifts: the romantic love between a husband and wife.

Set within the culture of ancient Israel, many of the expressions of adoration and desire may seem a bit odd; such as her neck being like a tower (4:4) or her flowing hair like a flock of goats (4:1; 6:5) or her belly like a "heap of wheat" (7:2). That hardly matches the unrealistic body image foisted by our present culture.

The real contrasts, though, are even more startling: the beauty and pleasure and even innocence of sexual desire as played out between a husband and wife as an expression of their great devotion to each other as compared to our culture's twisted, dirty, and ultimately very selfish view of sex.

"I am my beloved's and my beloved is mine" (Song of Sol. 6:3).

Perhaps I should have begun today's thoughts with a warning about its content, but no. Gifts from God don't carry warnings, only blessings.

16

Daily Bible Reading: Psalms 106; Proverbs 22:13-29

Real Heroes

Devotional Text: Psalm 106:23

It's not unusual to hear talk about heroes today. Usually it's men and women who put themselves in harm's way to serve and to protect citizens; you know, people like fire fighters, police officers, and soldiers.

It is admirable, is it not: ones who will go and do what others cannot or will not, all for the good of those served? Hero is an appropriate moniker.

We admire the courage of those willing to face danger and threat and peril. But that's nothing compared to what Moses did. He stood on behalf of Israel before the wrath of God.

Listen: "Therefore he said he would destroy them--had not Moses, his chosen one, stood in the breach before him, to turn away his wrath from destroying them" (Ps. 106:23).

Now there is a hero, he stood in the breach. He stood up for God's people who sinned and appealed for God's forgiveness (see Ex. 32:31-32).

Of course, even that brave act pales when we consider Jesus who not only "stood in the breach" but received the punishment of God's wrath for humanity's sin (2 Cor. 5:21; Heb. 2:9; 1 Pet. 2:24).

If we're going to use the word "hero" as we do, then not only does Moses exceed them, Jesus is the only real superhero.

17

Daily Bible Reading: Song of Solomon 7-8;
Lamentations 1; Hebrews 12:1-13

Who Should Change?

Devotional Text: Hebrews 12:1

We think God should be different.

Don't we?

Don't we think He should right all the wrongs, remove all the obstacles, and heal all the hurts? And if not for everyone, at least for me?

How about instead of God changing, we change?

What really needs to happen is for our thinking and understanding and perspective to be different.

The Bible says our need is for endurance (Heb. 12:1).

Endurance? That sounds like whatever the difficulty is, it's not going anywhere. I need to learn to deal with it.

Further, in the same place, the Bible says that it is because of God's discipline that we need to endure (12:7). And what's more, that discipline is "painful rather than pleasant" (v. 11).

Shall God change, or shall we?

18

Daily Bible Reading: Lamentations 2-3; Hebrews 12:14-29

Shining in Darkness

Devotional Text: Lamentations 3:22-24

The Lord's "steadfast love" never stops and "his mercies" never end. Every day they are new and fresh.

Can more encouraging, helpful, and hopeful words be found? And where they are found is itself insightful and amplifying. It's from a book devoted to lamenting, to mourning and sorrow. The words do seem out of place.

Listen to just a few verses prior: "He has made my teeth grind on gravel, and made me cower in ashes; my soul is bereft of peace; I have forgotten what happiness is; so I say, My endurance has perished; so has my hope from the Lord" (vv.16-18). This book is appropriately named.

So what is this ray of cheer doing in this middle of all this gloom? Remarkably, the writer introduces these beautiful words with, "Remember my affliction and my wanderings, the wormwood and the gall! My soul continually remembers it and is bowed down within me. But this I call to mind, and therefore I have hope" (vv. 19-21).

Here's the truth: sometimes life is bitter. Sometimes we are brought so low that happiness seems a distant memory at best. Yet God's love and mercy remain. Our present misery in no way negates His love and care. It's no reflection on the character of God, it's a reflection on the state of this wretched world and the ultimate destructiveness of sin.

So, not only are the words themselves beautiful, the darkness of their surroundings make them shine more brilliantly.

19

Daily Bible Reading: Lamentations 4; Isaiah 1; Hebrews 13

A Good Measuring Stick

Devotional Text: Hebrews 13:13

You cannot separate your relationship with God from your relationship with others. One cannot exist without the other.

Careless, thoughtless, inconsiderate treatment of fellow human beings is evidence of one who does not know God or His will. Ones who propose to give devotion to God yet disregard their neighbors are self-deceived.

Notice what happens at the end of Hebrews. It is helpful to remember that chapter divisions are not original in Scripture, but a helpful tool later added by men. That helpful tool can become a hindrance, though. Such is the case here.

Chapter twelve ends with this great charge, "let us offer to God acceptable worship, with reverence and awe, for our God is a consuming fire" (12:28-29). Then chapter 13 opens with loving your brother (v. 1), being hospitable to strangers (v. 2), remembering those in prison and ones mistreated (v. 3).

It's just that simple. You cannot honor God with reverence and awe without also loving and caring for the people you encounter in life: those you know and those you don't know.

So, a good and necessary measuring stick for your relationship with God is your treatment of others.

So, how do you measure up?

20

Daily Bible Reading: Isaiah 2-4; Ephesians 1:1-2:10

Am I Interested?

Devotional Text: Isaiah 2:14

We all know how easy it is to fall into a self-centered mode.

Before we know it, our whole manner of thinking and acting is focused on self. That's why Jesus said that denying self is a daily duty (Luke 9:23). We'd have to admit that it's an all-day-every-day kind of duty.

Did you ever consider how self-centered we can become even in our own Bible study? Does it ever happen that the only things that really catch our attention or pique our interest in our Bible reading are the things that directly apply or affect us?

For instance, Isaiah 2:14 is obviously a great prophetic passage of God's coming kingdom. It's repeated, nearly verbatim, in Micah 4:13. God is going to establish "the mountain of the house of the Lord." It will be "the highest of the mountains, and shall be lifted up above the hills" (v. 2). Obviously, this is of great importance to God.

For that, and no other reason, ought this also to be of great importance to me. What are its qualities? What will be characteristic of it? How does it affect humanity in general, and me in particular?

Is my interest piqued?

21

Daily Bible Reading: Isaiah 5-7; Ephesians 2:11-3:21

Privileged Information

Devotional Text: Ephesians 3:3-5

How about a little insider information? There are some people who are "in the know." They have access to information that all others have been denied. By virtue of that fact they possess a very valuable commodity.

How about some insider information from God? This is stuff that had been kept from man for generations. They did not and could not know it. But God made it known.

Specifically, He made it known to a very exclusive group, His holy apostles and prophets. And He did so through His own Holy Spirit.

Wow. That is some real insider information from very credible sources. But how could we ever hope to know what it is?

Ah, there's the question.

Well, Paul, one of those holy apostles, said that when we read what He has written we can know His insight "into the mystery of Christ" (Eph. 3:3-5).

What had previously been unknown and unknowable is now made known. It comes from the very mind of God. What began there was revealed by His own Spirit to the apostles and prophets and has been written so that in the Bible we possess the most important body of information known to humanity, period.

Really.

22
Daily Bible Reading: Isaiah 8-10; Ephesians 4:1-24

Need to Know

Devotional Text: Isaiah 8:19

People have long been fascinated with the "world beyond." Efforts to contact spirits or the dead or otherworldly beings and creatures captivates many. It always has.

It isn't that the Bible denies the reality of all of this. What God has a problem with is when people think that these are sources of information, knowledge and guidance. That is an affront to God.

"When they say to you, 'Inquire of the mediums and the necromancers ["fortunetellers" and "spiritualists"] who chirp and mutter,' should not a people inquire of their God? Should they inquire of the dead on behalf of the living?" (Isa. 8:19).

Indeed!

To be sure, there are things we want to know. There is information we would wish to possess. And we think that it is to be somehow found outside of this drab and common existence of ours. Why?

Instead, Isaiah urges, "Tell them, 'No, we're going to study the Scriptures.' People who try the other ways get nowhere--a dead end!" (Isa. 8:20; The Message).

The fact is God has given us what we need to know and all we need to know. Our pursuit of what is "out there" will prevent us from knowing what is right here, given by God.

23
Daily Bible Reading: Psalms 107-108; Proverbs 23:1-16

Don't You Do It!

Devotional Text: Proverbs 23:3,4,6,9,10,13

Some of my very best decisions have been to not do something I was pondering. I decided not to pass on a yellow line, or smart off to my parents, or go to that party, or ask that girl out on a date, or...well, you get the idea.

Wisdom includes not only doing what is right and good, but also not doing some things.

This portion of Proverbs begins several statements with, "Do not..."

Do not...
...desire his [a ruler's] delicacies, for they are deceptive food (v. 3).
...toil to acquire wealth; be discerning enough to desist (v. 4).
...eat the bread of a man who is stingy; do not desire his delicacies (v. 6).
...speak in the hearing of a fool, for he will despise the good sense of your words (v. 9).
...move an ancient landmark or enter the fields of the fatherless (v. 10).
...withhold discipline from a child (v. 13).

Just as important as knowing what to do is knowing what not to do.

24

Daily Bible Reading: Isaiah 11-14; Ephesians 4:25-5:21

Grieving God's Holy Spirit

Devotional Text: Ephesians 4:30

Many Bible students have pondered what it means to "not grieve the Holy Spirit of God" (Eph. 4:30). Certainly, we would not want to be guilty of such.

As is true with any challenging passage, various ideas and interpretations abound.

May I suggest not forgetting one of the fundamental rules of biblical interpretation: consider the context. As a matter of fact, it has been stated that context is the most important principle to determine meaning. I do not disagree.

The above-mentioned statement is found in the middle of a paragraph containing a whole series of practical admonitions, both positive and negative.
- Do not lie, but speak the truth with each other (v. 25).
- Do not allow your anger to become sin (v. 26).
- Do not steal, but work so you can share with others in need (v. 27).
- Be mindful of your language, let your words be gracious and edifying (v. 29).
- Do away with all bitterness, wrath, anger, clamor, slander, and malice (v. 31).
- Do be kind, tenderhearted, and forgiving (v. 32).

These instructions, like all Scripture, are given by God's Spirit. Failure to carry through on these very practical and personal matters would indeed grieve God and His Spirit.

25

Daily Bible Reading: Isaiah 15-19; Ephesians 5:22-6:24

Answerable to God

Devotional Text: Isaiah 15:1; 17:1; 18:1; 19:1

Unlike other daily devotional thoughts that derive from a single thought, verse, or maybe paragraph, today's comes from the entire Old Testament reading in Isaiah, all five chapters.

You may read from a Bible that provides headings over sections of Scriptures. Mine does. From those I can see that all of this portion of Isaiah is a series of oracles against the nations; specifically Moab, Damascus, Cush, and Egypt (though these section titles are not inspired, we know these are correct by noting 15:1; 17:1; 18:1; and 19:1).

It is more than just interesting that Isaiah, a prophet of God to Judah, is speaking out against these other nations. One might wonder, why would Isaiah be speaking like this to them? It's the simple fact that these nations, along with all other nations, are accountable to God. They are answerable to Him and will be judged (and were) by Him.

It seems a common thought today that the only people answerable to God are the ones who chose to believe in Him or who have at some time and in some way indicated they wish to follow Him.

Not so.

Not only is that clear here from Isaiah, but Jesus' own description of the judgment says that "before Him will be gathered all the nations, and He will separate people one from another as a shepherd separates the sheep from the goats" (Matt. 25:32).

I cannot conveniently excuse my accountability to my Creator.

26
Daily Bible Reading: Isaiah 20-23; Colossians 1:1-23

Pray More

Devotional Text: Colossians 1:3-4

Paul was a big prayer. If he did it as often as he claimed, and there is no reason to think otherwise, he spent copious amounts of time in the practice.

I need to pray more. That always has been and always will be true. I can learn a thing or two about it from Paul.

For instance, his opening words to the Christians at Colossae reference his prayers on their behalf. He thanks God every time since he had heard of their faith in Jesus and their love for the saints (Col. 1:3-4).

There's something I could be praying about--thanking God when I pray for fellow Christians and congregations of God's people. I could sure do more of that.

Further, he says he prays for them specifically on several points:
- that they be filled with the knowledge of God's will in all spiritual wisdom and understanding (1:9).
- that they would walk in a manner worthy of the Lord, fully pleasing to Him (1:10).
- that they be strengthened with all power, according to His glorious might (1:11).

There's a lot more I could be praying for on behalf of fellow Christians.

While I'm at it, I need to be praying for the same for myself.

27

Daily Bible Reading: Isaiah 24-26; Colossians 1:24-2:23

I Want Peace

Devotional Text: Isaiah 26:3

A favorite hymn of mine has long been "Peace, Perfect Peace." The older I get, the sweeter its thought becomes.

Among the many appellations of God's own Son is "Prince of Peace" (Isa. 9:6).

Paul's favored greeting to the saints coupled grace and peace (Rom. 1:7; 1 Cor. 1:3; etc.).

God's own kingdom is characterized by righteousness, joy, and peace (Rom. 14:17).

To be a son of God awaits the one who makes peace (Matt. 5:9).

We do not and cannot understand how, but God's peace stands guard over our hearts and minds in Jesus Christ (Phil. 4:7).

Our world is troubled, in need of peace; troubled nations, troubled economies, troubled families, troubled youths, troubled marriages, troubled minds, troubled churches, troubled souls.

So precious are these words of Isaiah: "You keep in perfect peace whose mind is stayed on you, because he trusts in you" (26:3).

"Peace be to you" (Jesus).

28

Daily Bible Reading: Isaiah 27-29; Colossians 3:1-17

How I Am

Devotional Text: Colossians 3:5

"That's just the way I am!"

Ever heard bad behavior excused that way?

Ever say it yourself?

While it may be true that we do have tendencies to act and think in certain ways and those ways may not always be good or appropriate, it is certainly no excuse for crass, selfish, ill-tempered, inconsiderate actions.

We are responsible for how we act and think. As a matter of fact, the Bible says there are some things in us that not only do we not allow free reign, but we need to kill. Their presence does not mean we have no responsibility for them. Just the opposite is actually true.

"Put to death therefore what is earthly in you" (Col. 3:5).

That "therefore" points back to what was just said. There we are urged to set our minds on things above, not on things that are on earth (v. 2).

The truth is, when we merely act out on what is "in us" it only evidences failure on our part to "seek the things that are above, where Christ is, seated at the right hand of God" (v. 1).

God does not want us to be "just the way we are." He wants us to be like Him.

29

Daily Bible Reading: Isaiah 30-32; Colossians 3:18-4:18

Tune In

Devotional Text: Isaiah 30:9

I remember television when I was growing up consisted of a choice of three channels in black and white. I know my parents can recall the first time a television was even brought into their homes. Today, it's a choice of literally hundreds of channels, the possibility of high definition displays and even the opportunity for programs available on-demand.

We can find just about anything we want to watch at any time we may wish to view it.

We don't have to settle for anything. We are in control. This is consumerism at its "finest."

That's just it with television. It's all about entertainment, to consume with our eyes and our minds what pleases us. Yes, there may be some educational value, but, really, it's all about giving me what I want when I want it. If I don't like what is on this channel, I have many, many others to choose from.

Has this trained us to think we can treat God the same way? Really, humanity has not needed the modern television experience to learn such behavior. The prophet Isaiah rebuked God's people as "children unwilling to hear the instruction of the Lord" (Isa. 30:9). "They say to the prophets, 'Do not prophesy to us what is right; speak to us smooth things, prophesy illusions'" (v. 10).

Ultimately. Eternally. Spiritually. We may choose to hear something else, but there is only one channel. Am I "tuned in" to what God has to say?

30

Daily Bible Reading: Psalms 109-112; Proverbs 23:17-35

At God's Right Hand

Devotional Text: Psalm 110:1

Here's a bit of Bible trivia for you: What Old Testament text is the most frequently quoted in the New Testament?

The answer is Psalm 110:1. "The Lord says to my Lord: Sit at my right hand, until I make your enemies your footstool."

This passage is cited in passages like Acts 2:32-33; 7:55; Rom. 8:34; Eph. 1:20; Heb. 1:13; 8:1; 10:12; 1 Pet. 3:22.

That may be a bit of trivia, but it is hardly trivial.

Consistently the opening words of this Psalm are used by New Testament writers to establish the fact of Jesus' resurrection from the dead and that He presently occupies the place of highest honor: reigning at God's right hand.

Think about how you think about Jesus. What thought most frequently comes to mind?

On the cross? Praying in the garden? Teaching the multitudes? Healing the sick and raising the dead?

There is not a thing wrong with any of those. But how often do we--and should we--set our minds "on things above, where Christ is, seated at the right hand of God" (Col. 3:1-2)?

OCTOBER

1
Daily Bible Reading: Isaiah 33-35, Philemon 1

There's a Good Reason Why

Devotional Text: Philemon

Why?

Why in the world, contained in the pages of Holy Writ, are we introduced to an individual of such spectacular inconsequence?

Onesimus is a nobody's nobody. For the time and place in which he lived, one simply could not be of less importance. As a slave he could occupy no lower place on the social strata, but at least he could provide service to his master. Now, as a runaway slave, even the little worth he had vanished.

Yet, there he is occupying the mind, the concern, and the pen of Paul in his brief letter to Philemon. He's actually the topic and occasion of the letter. Philemon's runaway slave has become his brother in Christ. Paul wishes him to receive Onesimus as the latter, not the former. This unfinished story is titillating. Did he, or didn't he?

The presence of this letter to Philemon and our introduction to Onesimus shouts clearly of God's compassion and care for even the very most insignificant, by our measure, not God's.

That also then means He cares for even me.

2

Daily Bible Reading: Isaiah 36-37; 1 John 1:1-2:6

A Good Question

Devotional Text: Isaiah 36:4

Asking the right question is important, but it's only half of the equation.

"On what do you rest this trust of yours?" (Isa. 36:4). That is a good question. The one asking it was the pagan king, Sennacherib, through his messenger. It was posed to the inhabitants of Jerusalem as the Assyrian army stood outside its walls.

Let's consider this situation. This was the highly successful Assyrian army fresh off of victories over all the other fortified cities of Judah as well as numerous other cities and nations (vv. 1, 19; 37:12-13). From all appearances, Assyria had the upper hand, and it would be utter foolishness to offer any resistance.

It seemed so obvious. The words of Sennacherib made sense: "Beware lest Hezekiah mislead you by saying, 'The Lord will deliver us'" (36:18). What is more, he asked the compelling question, "Has any of the gods of the nations delivered his land out of the hand of the king of Assyria? (36:18).

Of course, Sennacherib had never encountered the God of Israel. Neither did he account for the angel of the Lord. Hezekiah trusted God for deliverance despite the apparent odds. In response to the king's petition for help, God sent His angel, who slew 185,000 of Assyria's military. Sennacherib left. Jerusalem was saved.

Are we willing to stand against "obvious" odds and reasoned arguments against God and His will? Do we have the trust and confidence of Hezekiah? Sennacherib's question is a good one.

3

Daily Bible Reading: Isaiah 38-40; 1 John 2:7-29

Light or Dark?

Devotional Text: 1 John 2:9-10

"In the dark" is not a good place to be; that is, unless you are trying to sleep. But even then one is not alert to his surroundings. Figuratively speaking, being in the dark and being asleep are about the same thing.

Much more preferable is the light. We can see better. Everything is visible. Nothing is hidden or unknown. Decisions, thought processes, and understanding flourish in the light of day.

Jesus, appropriately, is called light. He's light because He is truth. He's light because He brings goodness and righteousness. Sadly, this dark world did not appreciate or even want the light that was Jesus Christ (John 3:19).

Before followers of Jesus get too comfortable or smug about their place in the light, we need to remember that darkness takes other forms than just ignorance, superstition, and wickedness. "Whoever says he is in the light and hates his brother is still in darkness.

Whoever loves his brother abides in the light" (1 John 2:9-10).

A key element to enlightenment is love for our brothers. So, how light, or dark, is it where you are?

4

Daily Bible Reading: Isaiah 41-42; 1 John 3

A New Word

Devotional Text: Isaiah 42:6

I recently learned a new word: monoethnism. I had to read it a couple of times because at first I thought it was "monotheism," a word with which I am familiar [it means "one God" and is used to describe the belief of the Jewish people as opposed to the nations who believed in many gods, that is, polytheism]. But that word didn't make sense in the sentence. I had to look up this new one.

But this was a problem. I had no physical dictionary that contained the word and even a couple of reputable online dictionary sources did not have a listing. There wasn't even a wikipedia entry for it. It's not that the word itself is hard; mono means one and "ethnism" refers to race. The best clue I had was that it was used to describe the attitude developed by the people of Israel. They came to believe that as the "chosen" race they were the only people in whom God had an interest. This thinking is seen in their derogatory attitude toward Gentiles. They considered them "dogs."

They seemed to have missed the point that their being chosen was to serve as "a light to the nations" (Isa. 42:6; see also 49:6; 51:4). His dealing with them was intended to show the rest of the world His greatness and goodness and draw them to Him, not exclude them.

This had always been God's intention. His calling Abraham and giving him promises had to do with "all the families of the earth" being blessed (Gen. 12:3). The tragic irony is that monoethnism is far from dead. People still fail to understand that God isn't picking out a race of people, but from all races those who come to Him through Jesus.

5

Daily Bible Reading: Isaiah 43-44; 1 John 4

A Reliable Test

Devotional Text. 1 John 4:1

Whom and what can you believe?

The Bible says don't believe everything you hear (1 John 4:1). Instead, test it to determine whether or not it's true.

Ah, but there's the rub! What is a good test? What is a trustworthy standard that will produce reliable outcomes? Not all tests are good. Appearance on the internet is not a good test of truthfulness, right?

John says that "Whoever knows God listens to us; whoever is not from God does not listen to us. By this we know the Spirit of truth and the spirit of error" (1 John 4:6).

That may sound a little bit like that "if it's on the internet it must be true" argument, but really it's not. Is there reason to believe John that he is "from God"? Absolutely.

He begins this letter by explaining that its message is based on what he not only heard but also saw with his eyes. It is that "which we looked upon and have touched with our hands, concerning the word of life... that which we have seen and heard we proclaim also to you" (1 John 1:1,3; see also Heb. 2:3-4 for a very similar assertion).

The bottom line here is that we can confidently test whatever we hear and whomever we hear it from, by the content of Scripture. As clichéd as that may sound, it is still true.

6

Daily Bible Reading: Isaiah 45-47; 1 John 5

Be Careful

Devotional Text: Isaiah 45:5-7, 18

It's like the old saying distinguishing major and minor surgery: "Major is what I have, minor is what you have."

My problems are big, yours are not. Mine are real, yours are imagined. Mine are a great challenge; you just need to get over yours.

Israel's big problem was false gods. That may not be my problem, but it's a real and serious problem.

That's why Isaiah repeatedly declares God's word: "I am the Lord, and there is no other, besides me there is no God" (45:5, 6, 7, 18).

Lest we get too smug about our fidelity to the one, true, living God, let's not forget that idolatry takes many forms. It's found in familiar places like covetousness and personal pride (Col. 3:5; Rom. 1:25). I can be quite idolatrous without any images.

House Building

Devotional Text: Proverbs 24:3-4

A house can be hard to build, especially if you've never done it. For someone with experience, it's not such a big deal.

Building a home, that's a supreme challenge even for the most experienced. Not impossible, but a challenge.

"By wisdom a house is built, and by understanding it is established; by knowledge the rooms are filled with all precious and pleasant riches" (Prov. 24:3-4).

The furnishings of a well-built home have nothing to do with furniture, floor coverings, window treatments, square footage, neighborhood location, or even quality of construction.

Wisdom and knowledge are key.

Remember the fear of the Lord is the beginning of wisdom and that the knowledge of God is the only trait worthy of boasting (Prov. 9:10; Jer. 9:23-24).

If you are to have a home, be sure it is very well built.

8
Daily Bible Reading: Isaiah 48-50; 2 John

Truth and Love

Devotional Text: 2 John 1:12

Whom do you love?

Besides the usual suspects like family and close friends, who are the objects of your fond affections?

That can be answered by the response to another question: What do you love?

John readily confessed his love for the "elect lady" and her "children" because of their love for the truth (2 John 1:12). He also knew that everyone else who loved the truth would also love them.

Love of the truth bound them all together in the Lord. After all, it is His own word that is truth (v. 4; John 17:17).

There is none of this "my" truth and "your" truth or relative, changing truth. No unclear, confusing, fluid and ambiguous talk here.

Truth comes from the Father, is quite knowable, can be followed, and is unchanging.

That is worth loving, as are those who also love it the same.

Daily Bible Reading: Isaiah 51-53; 3 John

Encouraging

Devotional Text: Isaiah 52:7

Fear mongers are everywhere. If it's not the economy, it's health care. If it's not health care, it's the elected officials. If it's not the elected officials, it's cultural immorality. If it's not...well, you get the idea.

Chicken Little protegés are in no short supply.

That's not to say there aren't some disturbing things going on in our world. The answer to fear mongering is not one's head stuck either in the sand or the Pollyanna sky.

But, no matter the circumstances, encouragement is always in order. Perhaps when times are most serious is when encouragers are most needed.

"How beautiful upon the mountains are the feet of him who brings good news, who publishes peace, who brings good news of happiness, who publishes salvation, who says to Zion, 'Your God reigns'" (Isa. 52:7).

Ultimate good news, of course, is the message of Jesus Christ and the ultimate encouragement is that God reigns.

I'm confident that the early church had its fear mongers as well. Interesting, though, that we don't know their names, only the name of the "son of encouragement," Barnabas (Acts 4:36).

This world could use fewer Chicken Littles and more Barnabases.

10
Daily Bible Reading: Isaiah 54-57; John 1:1-28

Whose Child?

Devotional Text: John 1:12-13

Whose child are you?

Of course, there's more than one way to answer that. I could say that I'm a child of Don and Mary. That's literally and physically true. I could also say I'm a child of the '70s.

There are unquestionable cultural influences that have shaped my thinking and outlook.

There is another, intriguing possibility, that is, being a child of God. It could be argued that everyone is that by virtue of being a part of the family of man. But, from God's perspective there is more to it than that.

"But to all who did receive him, who believed in his name, he gave the right to become children of God, who were born, not of blood nor of the will of the flesh nor of the will of man, but of God" (John 1:12-13).

They key to this, you'll notice, is the will of God. But the problem here is that God also gave each of us a will. The challenge is that only one will can prevail. Remember, Jesus taught us to pray that God's will be done (Matt. 6:10). That happens when our will is submitted to His and thereby we are born of God.

So, again, whose child are you?

301

11
Daily Bible Reading: Isaiah 58-60; John 1:29-51

Rite or Right?

Devotional Text: Isaiah 58:2

It's pretty simple, yet so difficult to get. To borrow from Mark Twain and alter for our own purposes it's not the parts of the Bible that are difficult that give us trouble, it's the ones easily understood.

So, much, much more important to God than our being religious, is our being like Him.

God's people appeared quite religious: "Yet they seek me daily and delight to know my ways, as if they were a nation that did righteousness and did not forsake the judgment of their God; they ask of me righteous judgments; they delight to draw near to God" (Isa. 58:2).

So what was God's complaint? "Behold, in the day of your fast you seek your own pleasure, and oppress all your workers. Behold, you fast only to quarrel and to fight and to hit with a wicked fist" (Isa. 58:3-4).

Instead, "Is not this the fast that I choose: to loose the bonds of wickedness, to undo the straps of the yoke, to let the oppressed go free, and to break every yoke? Is it not to share your bread with the hungry and bring the homeless poor into your house; when you see the naked, to cover him, and not to hide yourself from your own flesh?" (Isa. 58:6-7).

More important than the religious rite is doing right and being right.

12
Daily Bible Reading: Isaiah 61-64; John 2

Read the Signs

Devotional Text: John 2:11

Can you imagine a world without signs? Nothing to identify businesses or roads, no indications of speed limits or driving instructions or distances to upcoming destinations.

Signs can be for information, direction, instruction, warning, and yes, advertising. Signs make our world more understandable.

When Jesus turned water to wine at the wedding feast in Cana of Galilee, John says it was the "first of his signs" (John 2:11). All through his gospel John calls Jesus' miracles "signs."

Jesus' miracles, His signs, identified who He was. They made it clear that though He was one living among men, He was no mere man. It was the signs that directed men to believe on Him as the Christ, the Son of God and that through Him they might have life (John 20:31).

Can you imagine faith without signs?

13
Daily Bible Reading: Isaiah 65-66; John 3

The Footstool

Devotional Text: Isaiah 66:1

We have an ottoman in our house, as do many homes. It's a useful, functional little piece.

It hardly ranks up there with the sofa or recliner, but it's nice to have nonetheless. In case you don't know, ottoman is just a fancy name for a footrest or a footstool. It's the only item in the living room for which mother's advice of "Don't put your feet on the furniture" doesn't apply.

That gives a little perspective when the Bible says that the earth is God's footstool (Isa. 66:1). That's not the highest praise for terra firma, yet it is God's creation and it is functional and serves an important purpose.

By comparison, heaven is God's throne. There's the footstool, and then there's the throne.

We would do well to remember that. We don't want miss out on the throne for the lowly footstool.

We may live now on this earth, but the footstool isn't our home. It's not what we long for, it doesn't capture our fancy, and neither is it the object of our fondest affections.

Again, we don't want to miss the throne for the sake of the footstool.

14
Daily Bible Reading: Psalm 117-118; Proverbs 24:19-34

In the Middle

Devotional Text: Psalm 118:1, 29

Psalm 118 is a bit of a novelty in the Bible. It is found in the very middle of the Sacred Text. There are 594 chapters before it and 594 chapters after it. The shortest chapter precedes it, Psalm 117. The longest chapter follows it, Psalm 119.

While that is interesting, though a bit contrived, remember, chapter divisions (as well as verse divisions) are man-made, still, it's worth noting the center of the Bible.

Its opening and closing verses are identical: "Oh give thanks to the Lord, for he is good; for his steadfast love endures forever!" (vv. 1, 29).

Novelty or not, Psalm 118 communicates the heart of Scripture: that God is good and full of steadfast love and that thanking Him is the most important activity in which we may engage!

How central to my own life is the center of the Bible?

15
Daily Bible Reading: Jeremiah 1-2; John 4:1-42

Are My Advantages Advantageous?

Devotional Text: John 4:41

People with every advantage and the greatest opportunities sometimes fail, while successes can emerge from very unexpected sources. Life just works that way at times.

Think about the ready and receptive faith of the Samaritans. After Jesus' celebrated conversation with the Samaritan woman at the well of Sychar, she shared her exciting discovery with fellow townspeople. They too learned the identity of this Jewish visitor.

Jesus then stayed two days in their community and many "believed because of His word" (John 4:41).

Contrast that with Jews whom Jesus would soon rebuke for not only their lack of faith, but their insistence on signs and wonders (v. 48).

Jews who had every reason to believe did not (for the most part), and Samaritans with far less opportunity and none of the Jews' advantage believed based only on His word.

How does my own faith, or lack of it, correspond to my advantages and opportunities?

16

Daily Bible Reading: Jeremiah 3-4; John 4:43-5:15

It is Critical

Devotional Text: Jeremiah 3:7

It's obvious, but can I say it? Leadership is critical.

Jeremiah prophesied to God's people when they were on the skids. Their demise was imminent. Judah was described as "treacherous" (Jer. 3:7), and by comparison her sister, Israel (already long gone into Assyrian captivity), was "more righteous" than she (v. 11).

Despite how bad things were—and they were going to get worse—Jeremiah looked to a better time. One thing that would make it better is that God said, "I will give you shepherds after my own heart" (Jer. 3:15).

Poor leadership had brought them low, good leadership would restore their fortunes.

Two things come quickly to mind. One is that David was a "man after God's own heart" (Acts 13:22). That is requisite for an effective leader of God's people. Second, is that God's model of leadership throughout Scripture is shepherds.

Poor shepherds are detrimental to the flock. They contributed significantly to Judah's present trouble (see Jer. 23:1-4), and Jesus saw shepherd-less people as "harassed and helpless" (Matt. 9:36).

God knows His people's need and has always made provision for them to have shepherds (see Acts 20:28, Eph. 4:11; 1 Pet. 5:1-2). It's critical.

17
Daily Bible Reading: Jeremiah 5-6; John 5:16-47

The Problem With Growing Up

Devotional Text: John 5:19, 30

Remember as a child wanting to grow up? Wanting to do grown-up things and especially not having anyone tell you what to do? You could do whatever you wanted. That would be great.

Then you did grow up and the reality fell short of the expectation. Being grown up also meant being responsible, and it wasn't so much doing whatever you wanted but doing what had to be done because there was no longer anyone to do it for you. And what is more, now there are times when you just wish there were someone who would tell you what to do!

Wanting to be grown up gets replaced by wanting to be a kid again. Life is eminently unfair. It is remarkable to think about Jesus, the one who had all authority (to do whatever He pleased) and all wisdom (so He always knew what to do).

He said, "The Son can do nothing of his own accord, but only what he sees the Father doing. For whatever the Father does, that the Son does likewise." Further, "I can do nothing on my own. As I hear, I judge, and my judgment is just, because I seek not my own will but the will of him who sent me" (John 5:19, 30).

Life isn't about doing what I want, or what someone else tells me, unless what I want is to do God's will or that "someone else" is God.

18

Daily Bible Reading: Jeremiah 7-8; John 6:1-24

You Can't Get Over It

Devotional Text: Jeremiah 7:28

Some setbacks are temporary. Some losses can be overcome. Some defeats are not final.

Then there are the other kind.

A loss of truth is the insurmountable type.

Oh, it may not be immediate. It might appear that you'll get by. It may seem as though the truth was skirted, dodged, or broken with no real ill-effects.

It's an illusion.

The loss of truth cannot be survived.

Isaiah's warning is dire: "truth has stumbled in the public square" (Isa. 59:14). A few years later, his successor, Jeremiah, gives the inevitable and chilling pronouncement, "truth has perished" (Jer. 7:28).

Judah would not and could not recover.

No one could.

19

Daily Bible Reading: Jeremiah 9-10; John 6:25-71

It Matters

Devotional Text: John 6:27

Do you have a job? Do you work? Do you make money to provide for yourself and your loved ones?

It's the honorable and right thing to do. The Bible even says that if a person fails here he is worse than an unbeliever who has denied the faith (1 Tim. 5:8). Wow! How's that for strong language?

Now, let's take that one step further. Jesus tells us to "not work for the food that perishes, but for the food that endures to eternal life, which the Son of Man will give to you" (John 6:27).

He's talking about priorities. For all the effort we put into putting food on the table, so to speak, it is all "food that perishes," and not just the food but also the clothes, the house, the cars, the bank accounts, and all the goodies in our lives. They all will perish.

But what about what won't perish? What about the eternal? Will we "work" for that "food?" It's not as immediate, it's not as pressing, but it is, well, eternal.

Spiritual food, food that endures to eternal life, just doesn't matter that much to people in the face of daily life. The time is coming, though, when nothing will matter any more.

20
Daily Bible Reading: Jeremiah 11-13; John 7:1-24

Belonging to God

Devotional Text: Jeremiah 11:14

Belonging to God is not a complex matter. Neither is it a matter beyond our control.

We're not physically born into it or have it somehow thrust or imposed on us, nor is it reserved for theologians or the spiritually elite.

It has always been the same. Jeremiah touched on it in the Old Testament: "Listen to my voice, and do all that I command you. So shall you be my people, and I will be your God" (Jer. 11:4).

Jesus hit it in the New: "Why do you call me 'Lord, Lord,' and not do what I tell you?" (Luke 6:46).

Knowing that God will one day claim His own, then my present agenda becomes quite clear.

21

Daily Bible Reading: Psalms 119:1-64; Proverbs 25:1-18

Jesus and Proverbs

Devotional Text: Proverbs 25:6-7

Did Jesus use Proverbs? That is, was He familiar with and informed and guided by the book of Proverbs?

It shouldn't be surprising that He was.

Consider this Proverb and Jesus' own instruction: "Do not put yourself forward in the king's presence or stand in the place of the great, for it is better to be told, 'Come up here,' than to be put lower in the presence of a noble" (Prov. 25:6-7).

Jesus taught one should not seek out a place of honor at a wedding feast lest you get replaced by someone more important; rather, take the last place so that the one who invited you will say, "Friend, move up higher" (Luke 14:8-10). "For everyone who exalts himself will be humbled, and he who humbles himself will be exalted" (Luke 8:11).

Jesus knew the wisdom of Proverbs, so ought we.

22

Daily Bible Reading: Jeremiah 14-16; John 7:25-53

Not So Common Knowledge

Devotional Text: John 7:27, 41-42

Sometimes what we think we know keeps us from knowing what we should know.

Why didn't everyone who encountered Jesus believe in Him? Part of it was because of what they thought they knew about the coming Christ. Note John 7:27, 41-42. Their ignorance masqueraded as knowledge.

Then when someone with knowledge spoke up, in this case Nicodemus, he was ridiculed for not knowing what they "knew" (see vv. 45-52).

Knowledge comes in a couple of varieties: what is commonly accepted, and is quite often wrong, and then what is genuine. The genuine is frequently rejected for no other reason than it doesn't fit common knowledge.

Jesus' problem was that He wasn't the former, but He was the latter.

My problem is avoiding the former and pursuing the latter.

23
Daily Bible Reading: Jeremiah 17-18; John 1:8-30

Doing It Wrong

Devotional Text: Jeremiah 17:1

You're doing it wrong.

That's all that could be said about God's people in Jeremiah's day. The word of God that was to be written on their hearts was not there (Ps. 40:8), instead it was their own sin, written with an iron pen with a diamond point (Jer. 17:1). Their children, instead of knowing the Law of God (Deut. 6:6-7), remembered only their false gods (Jer. 17:2).

It's not difficult to know what is genuinely precious and important to anyone. It's not what they say or claim Not that people are intentionally deceitful, but the heart, even one's own heart, is easily deceived (Jer. 17:9).

Two easy criteria are these: what is on one's heart and what is important to one's children.

Jesus said that knowing one's heart is as simple as following their money. It goes where their heart resides. Does it go to self to get more and better things? Does it go to entertainment and pleasure? Where we spend our money is a no-fail indicator of our heart's affections (Matt. 6:21).

As for children, they tend to mimic their parents' behaviors and values. They're righteous because they are taught, trained and led to be so. They are not for the same reasons.

So, considering my own heart and children, if I have them, am I doing it wrong?

24

Daily Bible Reading: Jeremiah 19-22; John 8:31-59

Only Jesus

Devotional Text: John 8:33

To put it bluntly, they had no need for Jesus. At least they didn't think so.

The offer of freedom to Jesus' Jewish contemporaries held little sway. "How is it that you say, 'You will become free'?" (John 8:33).

Their mistaken belief was that being Abraham's offspring punched their spiritual ticket.

As such, "we have never been enslaved to anyone." Really? Had they forgotten Egypt and Babylon?

Not only did they suffer from selective amnesia, they were oblivious to their need for freedom from sin that enslaves all men (vv. 34-36).

Things really have not changed much in that people still don't see their need for what Jesus alone can offer. His words of knowing the truth and the truth making one free (v. 32) are applied in all sorts of situations. But it is rarely in the one that Jesus used them: being His disciple and being freed from sin.

Jesus' is not just another voice on the religious landscape, another version of the same thing in the marketplace of faiths.

Any variety of faiths may offer the same lessons about living life, but only Jesus Christ can free us from enslavement to sin.

Only Jesus.

25
Daily Bible Reading: Jeremiah 23-24; John 9

An Important Pair

Devotional Text: Jeremiah 23:5

Can you complete the following pairings? peanut butter and _____; _____ and cheese; Abbott and _____; salt and _____; _____ and arrow; justice and _____

Some things just go together. Right?

That last one might be a bit tricky. But biblically speaking, justice has a partner; it's righteousness. Not only are they a matched set, they form a major theme of Bible thought.

God chose Abraham as one to keep His way by "doing righteousness and justice" (Gen. 18:19). David's exceptional reign as Israel's king was distinguished by the administration of justice and righteousness (2 Sam. 8:15). The visiting queen of Sheba knew Solomon's reign was to be exactly the same (1 Kings 10:9). And guess what serves as the foundation of the Lord's throne? Yep, justice and righteousness (Ps. 89:14; 97:2).

As the prophets called God's people to return to faithfulness to Him, they lamented this pair's absence and prophesied its return. "Behold, the days are coming, declares the Lord, when I will raise up for David a righteous Branch, and he shall reign as king and deal wisely, and shall execute justice and righteousness in the land (Jer. 23:5; not to mention numerous other such references in Jeremiah, Isaiah, and Ezekiel, plus Hosea, Amos, Micah, and Zephaniah).

To paraphrase, a primary Bible emphasis is to do what is right and what is fair. That only leaves the question: is the Bible's emphasis also my emphasis?

316

26

Daily Bible Reading: Jeremiah 25-26; John 10

Whose Agenda?

Devotional Text: John 10:10

What is your agenda?

We all have one. We're out to accomplish something, get something, do something, become something. It affects everything we do if not every thought we think and every word we say.

At the same time, we are also affected by others' agendas. Some people are quite effective manipulators and can influence others to participate in their own agendas.

Agendas are not always obvious and can even be quite deceitful.

That's important to know when it comes to Satan. He promises lots of pleasure and enjoyment, if not happiness itself. These are acquired, according to Him, through any number of means that differ from God's word and will. In spite of what he may promise, Jesus says "the thief [Satan] comes only to steal and kill and destroy" (John 10:10). That is his agenda.

Jesus has one too. That is to give life and to provide it abundantly (John 10:10). That is also true in spite of Satan's claims about Him.

So, whose agenda is at work in my life?

27

Daily Bible Reading: Jeremiah 27-29; John 11:1-44

Am I Prepared for God's Plan?

Devotional Text: Jeremiah 29:11

"'For I know the plans that I have for you,' declares the Lord" (Jer. 29:11).

It must be reassuring to know that God has plans for us. I see this passage quoted and posted frequently. The quotation is often continued, "plans to prosper you and not to harm you, plans to give you hope and a future" (NIV).

These words are used to help people endure difficult and uncertain times.

Here is what is rarely ever said about this text: Jeremiah is telling people of Israel who have already been taken captive to Babylon to settle in, to build houses and plant gardens, get married and raise families and get acclimated to the city to which they have been exiled (vv. 47).

Why? Because they are going to be there for 70 years! Only then will God "visit you, and I will fulfill to you my promise and bring you back to this place" (v. 10). Only then comes the familiar line, "For I know the plans I have for you..."

Like it or not, sometimes God's plan for us is not at all what we want. In this case it was to remain in less-than-desirable circumstances. So too might be His plans for us.

That's probably not what we want to hear and not what those exiles wanted to hear either.

Are we really ready to know God's plans for us?

28

Daily Bible Reading: Psalms 119:65-120; Proverbs 25:19-26:9

It's All Good

Devotional Text: Psalm 119:68

Sometimes the most profound truths are the most simply stated.

Such is the case with Psalm 119:68, "You are good and do good."

Mothers encourage their children to be good boys and girls. Conscientious kids try to be what momma wants them to be. They don't always succeed.

God doesn't make an effort to be good, He is good. And because He is good, what God does is good.

That may give us trouble. We see things happen in this world that do not appear to be good. The Bible even talks about God doing things that don't seem to us to be good.

Here's the dilemma: will we attempt to alter God's actions so they fit our definition of good, or will we adjust our understanding, knowing that God, being good, does good?

Simple, but not easy.

29

Daily Bible Reading: Jeremiah 30-31; John 11:45-12:11

For or Against God?

Devotional Text: John 11:53

It's kind of hard to believe that someone who intended to serve God would actually wind up working against Him instead.

It happened among the leading religious rulers of Jesus' day. They came to an official decision to eliminate Jesus (see John 11:53). They readily acknowledged that Jesus was performing many miraculous "signs" and, as a result, they thought that "everyone will believe in Him." Their fear was that "the Romans will come and take away both our place and our nation" (vv. 47-48).

It was God's intention that all men would believe in Him (John 6:29). It was the religious rulers' intention that the nation be maintained (see v. 48). The very thing God wanted they perceived as a threat to what they wanted.

Here they were, the supposed leaders of God's people, at cross-purposes with God.

Instead of thinking, "Those poor chief priests and Pharisees," we should think, "Are my intentions, purposes, and desires aligned with God's or at odds with Him?"

Don't think it could never happen to me.

30
Daily Bible Reading: Jeremiah 32-33; John 12:2-50

I Can't See It

Devotional Text: Jeremiah 32:35

A common complaint regarding God has more to do with our own weakness and failure, rather than any shortcoming of His.

People often say, "Well, I just don't see how God can..."you finish the sentence. Our inability to comprehend what God has done or is doing is not an indictment against God, but against us.

God brought the Babylonians to Jerusalem for the express purpose of overthrowing it and taking the citizens as captives. Now, from the Jews' perspective this was absolutely incomprehensible. Jeremiah's message to King Zedekiah was to not fight the Babylonians because God was giving him into the Chaldean king's hand. He said flatly, "If you fight against the Chaldeans you will not succeed" (Jer. 32:35).

In light of these bewildering circumstances, twice the affirmation is made, once as a statement and once as a redundant question-"Nothing is too difficult for You" (Jer. 32:17; see also v. 27).

When we just can't see how God can do something, that is an encouragement rather than a discouragement. He is greater than are we. There is so much we cannot see and do not know. But for God, His abilities have no end.

God is not limited by our ability, or rather inability, to see.

31

Daily Bible Reading: Jeremiah 34-36; John 13:1-17

Working in Ignorance

Devotional Text: John 13:7

"You do not understand."

That can be hard to take. We may think someone is being harsh and unkind when they say that, like they're calling us stupid.

When Jesus told Peter he didn't understand, He wasn't being unkind (John 13:7). He was just stating a fact. Peter was not rightly comprehending Jesus' actions when He proceeded to wash the disciples' feet on the occasion of the Last Supper. First he refused that his Master would perform such a menial task on him and then, hearing Jesus say that if He didn't Peter had no "share" with Him, he wanted even more, wash my hands and head too!

Jesus assured him that understanding would come later.

For all of Peter's impetuous deeds, speaking before he thinks, and bold assertions of his own faithfulness, he becomes a central figure in the life of the early church, providing courageous and inspiring leadership for years to come. He did come to understand.

The point is that there may be, and likely are, some things we don't presently understand. We should not allow our current ignorance and inexperience to become an obstacle to future spiritual contributions we might make.

We should be patient. We should be persistent. We should humbly continue our service to God, ignorance notwithstanding.

NOVEMBER

1

Daily Bible Reading: Jeremiah 37-38; John 13:18-38

Following God is Hard

Devotional Text: Jeremiah 38:6

This isn't very easy to say. It can be very hard to take. But, doing what God tells us to do can make our lives miserable.

Jeremiah had faithfully proclaimed God's message, and what did he get for his troubles? He was jailed in a cistern with no water, lowered by ropes, and "Jeremiah sank in the mud" (Jer. 38:6).

John the Baptist boldly challenged Herod's sinfulness and literally lost his head (Matt. 14:10).

Paul tirelessly traveled and preached. As a result he was beaten, stoned, shipwrecked, adrift at sea, robbed, among many other dangers and hardships (2 Cor. 11:23-27).

This reality could be more than discouraging, especially if we lose sight of the fact that this life and this world are not what it's all about. If they were, it just wouldn't be worth it.

But what is real and what is important and what is of value is also what is invisible and eternal. Any hardship we may face in this life is momentary and light, no matter if it's mud, beatings, or beheading, because the glory God has in store for us is beyond all comparison (2 Cor. 4:17).

Just don't lose sight.

2

Daily Bible Reading: Jeremiah 39-41; John 14

I Have a Question

Devotional Text: John 14:6

I am glad people ask questions. Questions provide an opportunity for instruction, investigation, and enlightenment.

Sometimes people don't want to ask questions because they "might look dumb." If it weren't for some of the apostles' questions we might have missed out on some of Jesus' greatest teaching. In the upper room Thomas, Philip, and Judas (not Iscariot) all asked questions.

In response to Thomas we hear, "I am the way, and the truth, and the life. No one comes to the Father except through Me" (John 14:6).

To Phillip's suggestion, Jesus said, "Whoever has seen Me has seen the Father" (John 14:9).

And to Judas's inquiry the response is, "If anyone love Me, he will keep My word"(John 14:23).

Next time you don't know, ask. There is no telling how many people will be helped by the answer to your question.

We are deeply indebted to some inquisitive apostles.

3

Daily Bible Reading: Jeremiah 42-44; John 15

A Bigger God

Devotional Text: Jeremiah 42:6

We want our God to be all-powerful and all-knowing. We want Him to be great and mighty. That's what God is supposed to be.

We just don't want Him to be "bigger" than us.

Really, it's true.

Before the objections get too loud, what happens when God says what we don't like or what we don't want to hear?

Are we not like the people who told Jeremiah, "Whether it is good or bad, we will obey the voice of the Lord our God" (Jer. 42:6)? Then, when Jeremiah told them what God said, they replied, "You are telling a lie" (Jer. 43:2).

They wanted God to tell them to do what they wanted to do. When He didn't, they rejected His message, His messenger, and Him. They wanted God to answer to them, not themselves to Him.

Since God is bigger than are we, His ways and His thoughts are higher-much higher-than ours (Isa. 55:8-9). Since that is true, then undoubtedly God is going to do and say some things we do not like or want. Will we allow Him to remain "bigger" than us and will we submit to Him, even in things we don't like? Or will we insist that our own ways and our own thoughts remain supreme?

Are we really willing for God to be "bigger"?

4

Daily Bible Reading: Psalms 119:121-176; Proverbs 26:10-28

Positively Negative

Devotional Text: Proverbs 26:10-12

I dislike negativity.

I fight being negative myself and feel drained and weakened in the presence of others with negative spirits.

Some negativity, though, is necessary. The power of magnetism and electricity are based on the presence of both positive and negative.

Wise living, the theme of Proverbs, also demands the presence of negatives. Just as surely as we must know what to pursue in life, we must also know what and whom to avoid, and why. As anticipated, Proverbs provides these negatives.

Today's reading emphasizes negatives. Those identified are the fool (Prov. 26:10-12; see also vv. 19), the sluggard (lazy, slothful; vv. 13-16), the meddler (17), the deceiver (18-19, 23, 24-26), the whisperer (20, 22), the quarrelsome (21), the hurtful (27), and the liar (28).

A life lived wisely is not all positive. Is mine sufficiently negative?

5

Daily Bible Reading: Jeremiah 45-48; John 16

Falling Down

Devotional Text: John 16:1

I have tendencies toward physical instability.

In other words, I'm a klutz.

Much to my mother's chagrin, I was the kid with the constantly grass-stained knees, torn jeans, scraped hands and elbows, and a plethora of bumps and bruises.

Falling typically has negative outcomes. That's a spiritual as well as physical reality.

So, Jesus took preventative measures for His followers. "I have said all these things to you to keep you from falling away" (John 16:1).

That sounds very similar to John's statement, "My little children, I am writing these things to you so that you may not sin" (1 John 2:1). And also Peter's: "Therefore, brothers, be all the more diligent to make your calling and election sure, for if you practice these qualities you will never fall" (2 Pet. 1:10).

Two things we should take from all of this: One is to be greatly encouraged knowing how the Lord has provided everything for our spiritual well-being; and two, when we do fall, and we will, we know that it is not because God has failed us. He's made every provision. So much so, that from His perspective and because of what He's done and what He's provided, we should never fall.

6

Daily Bible Reading: Jeremiah 49-50; John 17

It's Not New

Devotional Text: Jeremiah 49:1

The "new" definition of tolerance suggests that it's OK for different people to believe different things, but it is NOT OK for one of them to attempt in any way to suggest that other's beliefs should change.

That would be fine if there were no absolute truth. The only way for there to be no absolute truth is for there to be no God. And if there is no God, well, then it's all a moot point anyway because we don't even exist without Him. That's not my point here, though.

Notice the subject matter of Jeremiah 49 and 50. God is pronouncing judgments against many nations Ammon, Edom, Damascus, Kedar and Hazor, Elam, and mostly Babylon.

These were nations who did not believe in the God of Israel, but they were still answerable to Him. He stood in judgment over them no matter what they believed or what gods they served.

Here is the point, my judgment is not dependent on my beliefs; that is, I'm not only accountable for who or what I believe in. Instead, my judgement is dependent on the fact that God is. He is absolute and I, as one of His creation, answer to Him.

So "new" isn't the right descriptor for what passes as tolerance today; rather, it's "wrong."

7

Daily Bible Reading: Jeremiah 51; John 18:1-18

Step Forward

Devotional Text: John 18:4

"Jesus fully realized all that was going to happen to him, so he stepped forward to meet them" (John 18:4; NLT).

Undoubtedly there are events at play at this point in John's gospel on a grand, make that the grandest, scale. The critical events procuring the salvation of humanity from sin are unfolding. God's plan formulated even prior to creation is on the verge of climax. Jesus has just spent several precious hours in final preparation for his apostles in an upper room and alone in agonizing prayer in the garden. Now, the betrayer is on his way. Ahead awaited injustice, hatred, ignorance, violence, agony, brutality, shame, and death.

At this moment, fully knowing all that was going to happen, Jesus stepped forward to meet them.

Remarkable.

On a much smaller scale, we may also confront hardships, challenges, struggles, and heartaches. It's much easier to avoid, retreat, skirt, and dodge. But, like Jesus, in whose steps we follow, we must step forward to meet whatever it is that lies ahead.

8

Daily Bible Reading: Jeremiah 52; Ezekiel 1; John 18:19-40

It Happened

Devotional Text: Jeremiah 52:12-16

It happened.

As unbelievable as it was; as sure as so many were that it could never be; as unpleasant and as unthinkable as anything anyone could imagine, it happened.

Exactly what Jeremiah had been prophesying happened.

For the record, it was on the tenth day of the fifth month of the nine-teenth year of the reign of Nebuchadnezzar, king of Babylon, that he entered Jerusalem, burned the house of the Lord, broke down the walls of Jerusalem and carried away the last of the Jews as captives to Babylon (52:12-16).

The deed was done. Jeremiah's despicable message had been right all along. The people he had been warning found lots of reasons to believe this troublemaker was mistaken. Finding fault with the prophet and his message was an easy game. It was also wrong.

Disregarding God's message is as popular today as it was among Jeremiah's constituents.

God's warnings against dishonesty and greed and anger and hatred and sexual promiscuity and homosexuality and drunkenness are largely disregarded. They are dismissed as the last vestiges of a puritanical past.

Just as surely as the Chaldean king marched into the holy city, the wrath of God will come because of precisely these cherished sins (Eph. 5:6).

9

Daily Bible Reading: Ezekiel 2-4; John 19:1-22

What to Do With Truth

Devotional Text: John 19:4,6

Truth is one thing. What you do with it, or because of it, is something else.

During Jesus' trial, Pilate gave voice to humanity's confusion-unjustified confusion, but confusion nonetheless--when he asked, "What is truth?" (John 18:38).

Immediately he then announced a truth: Jesus was innocent. He did so, not just once, but three distinct times (18:38; 19:4,6). Pilate did not fully realize just how true that was. He was not only innocent of the charges filed against Him, He was without sin, period.

As such He was fully undeserving of any type or form of punishment or even ill-treatment. Yet, Pilate proceeded to have Jesus flogged (an especially brutal and violent event which many victims did not survive). The soldiers under his charge mocked, insulted, beat on Him. Pilate vainly and repeatedly attempted to so placate the Lord's accusers that they might desist. Nothing worked.

Pilate knew the truth of Jesus' innocence. What he did with that truth was as though it was no truth at all.

What am I doing with the truth I know?

10
Daily Bible Reading: Ezekiel 5-7; John 19:23-42

When Will You Know It?

Devotional Text: Ezekiel 5:13

How do we know that God is God?

I don't think I would have ever thought to ask that question were it not for Ezekiel. Eight times (in today's reading), speaking for the Lord, he says that the people will know that He is the Lord (5:13; 6:7,10,13,14; 7:4,9,27). Eight times!

Incidentally, he says it 63 times throughout the book.

Here's the deal; Ezekiel is not just talking about being aware that God is deity. He's talking about recognizing and appreciating and comprehending that God is sovereign, that He rules over all, that all of humanity is answerable to Him.

What was it that was going to bring this point home to them? The fact that God's judgment and punishment was brought against them. Then the realization would come to them. Then they would comprehend.

It's not unlike when Paul says there will be a time when everyone, without exception, will confess the Lordship of Jesus Christ (Phil. 3:11). When will that be? At His revelation in the end.

The time is coming when all will know that God is God. No atheists, no agnostics, no doubters.

How much better to know God is God now than to only come to know it then.

11
Daily Bible Reading: Psalms 120-124; Proverbs 27:1-18

The Wrong Kind of People

Devotional Text: Psalm 120:6

It is said that every person is basically the average of the five people with whom they spend the most time. In other words, we are influenced, for good or ill, by the people we are around. We tend to become like what and whom we spend much time around.

That's why the Bible says that bad company ruins good morals (1 Cor. 15:33) and that people who pursue vanity become vain (2 Kings 17:15).

Surely, this is behind the cry of Psalm 120:6, "Too long have I had my dwelling among those who hate peace."

Since we cannot help but be affected by those we spend time with, maybe an evaluation of those people and their influences would be in order. Take a long serious look.

Whether it's by choice or not, the fact remains that these people are what you are becoming like. What are their attitudes and perspectives? Are they encouragers or discouragers? Do they tend toward spirituality or worldliness? Are their values and priorities aligned with God's? Do they see opportunities and blessings in life or are they always focused on the negatives?

Has it been too long that you've had your dwelling among the wrong kind of people?

12
Daily Bible Reading: Ezekiel 8-10; John 20

Grasping Truth

Devotional Text: John 20:8-9

A healthy dose of self-doubt is a good thing.

I'm not talking about always questioning oneself and having no confidence or self-assurance. But rather always recognizing the fact that I may be wrong.

One who thinks they already know and already have it all figured out is one who has ceased to learn.

A love for the truth demands that we always pursue it and don't camp on the idea that truth is equivalent with what I already understand and believe.

Consider the apostles' initial response to the resurrection of Jesus. The first report they received came from Mary Magdalene; at the time-she being a woman--this was considered a dubious source at best. In response, Peter and John ran to and investigated the empty tomb personally.

It is about this experience that the Bible says that John "saw and believed." But then, this statement: "For as yet they did not understand the Scripture, that he must rise from the dead" (John 20:8-9).

Jesus' resurrection was a matter of truth; it was in the Scripture (see also John 2:22), but the apostles had yet to grasp it.

Is there truth-already right there in the Scriptures-that I have yet to grasp?

13
Daily Bible Reading: Ezekiel 11-12; John 21

It's Not Over

Devotional Text: Ezekiel 11:20

When is it over? When is it too late? When is all hope gone?

And no, it has nothing to do with the intonations of a proverbial portly female.

All kidding aside, this is serious business. Doom and gloom spread quickly when we find ourselves in a hard spot. Circumstances are not only less than optimal, nothing is as we would want it or hope for it to be.

Consider those Israelites hauled off as captives to Babylon. Could anything have been worse for God's "chosen people"? Many thought it was over. They believed that was just how it would be from then on.

Then Ezekiel delivered a startling message. God said, "And they shall be My people, and I will be their God" (Ezek. 11:20). This was the language of the covenant going all the way back to Sinai. This was God's purpose and intent with Israel all along.

It was not over!

No matter how bad it then appeared, no matter how hopeless and impossible, God was not through with His people. His plan had not died.

Israel did not give up. Neither can we.

14
Daily Bible Reading: Ezekiel 13-15; 1 Timothy 1

Narrow Minded

Devotional Text: I Timothy 1:3

Wow, Paul must have been pretty narrow-minded. His first instruction to Timothy in his first letter was for him to stop certain teachers (1 Tim. 1:3). Was Paul really so intolerant or was he just arrogant and insecure? Or, was it something else?

His stated reason is that the opposed teaching promoted speculation rather than the "stewardship from God that is by faith" (1 Tim. 1:4).

What was the "stewardship from God"? Comparing translations can sometimes help clarify a text's meaning; this is not one of those instances. Comparisons give you things like, "administration of God," or "God's work," "God's ordered way of life" or "God's redemptive plan," or "divine training." Obviously translators struggle a bit here.

I found this note helpful: "The basic word (oikonomia) denotes the work of a household steward or manager or the arrangement under which he works: 'household management.' As a theological term it is used of the order or arrangement by which God brings redemption through Christ" (NET Bible notes).

So, yes, Paul was quite narrow-minded. He believed that preaching and teaching should promote and remain consistent with God's plan, arrangements, and purpose for mankind's redemption through Jesus by faith. Anything else should not be tolerated.

Stated another way: "Therefore I consider all your precepts to be right; I hate every false way" (Ps. 119:128).

15

Daily Bible Reading: Ezekiel 16; 1 Timothy 2

Where Did You Come From?

Devotional Text: Ezekiel 16:2

My parents asked me, "Were you born in a barn?" I don't think so. I was told it was St. Vincent's Hospital, and I have believed it.

Of course, the question was facetious. They knew and I knew I was not birthed in a barn. However, some uncouth, unthoughtful, or uncaring act on my part had suggested that my origins were of a less-than-refined or civilized nature.

Actions reflect origins. That is why God said of Jerusalem, "your father was an Amorite and your mother a Hittite" (Ezekiel 16:2). That was not a compliment.

God had directed Israel to overthrow the Amorites and the Hittites when they took possession of the promised land. Two purposes were served: one was God's judgment against these nations for their extreme wickedness and the other was so they would not be able to influence His own people in their evil ways.

But guess what, by their behavior, the people of Jerusalem appeared more to be the children of the Amorites and Hittites than God's children.

Peter also knew that actions reflect origins. "And if you call on him as Father...conduct yourselves with fear" (1 Pet. 1:17).

16

Daily Bible Reading: Ezekiel 17-18; 1 Timothy 3

The Truth and the Church

Devotional Text: 1 Timothy 3:15

Does the truth make the church the church or does the church make truth the truth?

Confused?

Think about it this way: Does the school make the student a student or does the student make the school a school?

It's the latter, is it not? A student is a student whether there is a school or not. And is a school that has no students really a school? Just because a child is in a school, does that make her a student? A school becomes a school when it is occupied by students.

Back to our original question: the relationship between church and truth is important. It is frequently confused. The "household of God...the church of the living God" is "a pillar and buttress of the truth" (bulwark, foundation, support; 1 Tim. 3:15).

The truth does not originate or derive from the church; the church, rather, becomes such because it is founded upon, practices, and proclaims the truth.

So, it is the truth that makes the church the church.

17
Daily Bible Reading: Ezekiel 19-20; 1 Timothy 4

Right Now

Devotional Text: Ezekiel 20:3

Carpe diem!

Even non-Latin speakers, such as myself, know what that means. We have lots of sayings about taking advantage of opportunities as they present themselves. Most of them are more folksy and common--and in English: "Strike while the iron is hot", "Make hay while the sun shines."

Few things are as tragic as missed opportunities.

The greatest of all opportunities is to seek God. So, conversely, the greatest tragedy is to miss that opportunity. It's like David told his son, Solomon, "if you seek Him, He will let you find Him" (1 Chron. 28:9). God wants to be found. But our search cannot be a casual, half-hearted enterprise. Rather, it is "with all your heart" and "diligently" (Jer. 29:13; Prov. 8:17).

But not only that, it has to be while we have the opportunity. So it was when leaders of God's people came to Ezekiel and God told him to tell them, "Is it to inquire of me that you come? As I live, declares the Lord God, I will not be inquired of by you" (Ezek. 20:3).

God was not being harsh. These people had long rejected God. Now judgment had come, and they were in captivity in Babylon. Seeking God was no longer an option

Right now is the time. Today is the day.

Carpe diem!

18

Daily Bible Reading: Psalms 125-129; Proverbs 27:19-28:9

The Heart as a Mirror

Devotional Text: Proverbs 27:19

Have you ever been surprised by what you learned about someone you thought you knew pretty well? It happens.

The fact is, what we "know" about people is often very superficial. We see and get to know their "public persona," how they choose to let themselves be known. We call it a "front" or a "mask."

That doesn't mean that this is all we can know.

"As in water face reflects face, so the heart of man reflects the man" (Prov. 27:19).

Water, like a mirror, is only going to reflect what is there. It can't change it or alter it; it is what it is. And so is the heart of a man.

That leaves us wondering how we can see someone's heart. God said that "man looks on the outward appearance but the Lord looks on the heart" (1 Sam. 16:7).

Jesus said there is a very reliable insight into a person's heart: "Where your treasure is, there your heart will be also" (Matt. 6:21).

If you want to find a person's heart, locate their money.

19

Daily Bible Reading: Ezekiel 21-22; 1 Timothy 5

Godliness

Devotional Text: 1 Timothy 5:4

What do you think of when you hear the word "godliness"? What does it mean to be "godly"?

We might be thinking in terms of depth of spirituality or a worshipful attitude or maybe great doctrinal truths. Maybe it's something like when Paul writes, "Great indeed, we confess, is the mystery of godliness" (1 Tim. 3:16).

We may begin to get the idea it's just something beyond us ordinary folks.

If so, we'd be wrong.

Godliness has a very practical side. Like when in 1 Timothy 5, Paul gives instructions about the church's care for widows. He says the first responsibility to these women, though, lies with family members: "[L]et them first learn to show godliness to their own household" (1 Tim. 5:4).

It is godly to take care of our family. It is godly to fulfill our duties and responsibilities. It is godly to serve.

Godliness is not reserved for the spiritually elite. It's for me and you.

20

Daily Bible Reading: Ezekiel 23; 1 Timothy 6

Not Behind My Back

Devotional Text: Ezekiel 23:25

Where do you keep your valuables?

Remember not everything that is valuable to you has the same worth with others. So, some valuables you may keep under lock and key or hidden away. Others you may display in a prominent or conspicuous location.

The point is, whatever we value, we honor it in an appropriate way.

That being said, what have you done with God? Is it appropriate relative to His value?

To Israel, he said, " [Y]ou have forgotten Me and cast Me behind your back" (Ezek. 23:35).

That is not appropriate; and it had happened before. It was a sin Jeremiah identified and also the sin of wicked king Jeroboam (Jer. 2:27; 1 Kings 14:9).

In response to such, God said, "I will show them My back and not My face in the day of their calamity" (Jer. 18:17). That is, as opposed to, "The Lord make His face to shine upon you and be gracious to you" (Num. 6:25).

God has a place, and it is not behind my back; because the place I want is the one where His face shines on me.

21
Daily Bible Reading: Ezekiel 24-26; 2 Timothy 1

The Generational Commission

Devotional Text: 2 Timothy 1:5

We are quite familiar with God's plan for the spread of the faith geographically. He charged that the gospel would be taken to all nations, into all the world, to the whole creation (Matt. 28:19; Mark 16:15).

Less celebrated than the "great commission," but no less important, is God's plan to spread the faith temporally, that is through time. An example of that plan is mentioned when Paul says the "sincere faith" present in Timothy was first found in his mother and grandmother (2 Tim. 1:5).

Maybe we could call it the "generational" commission.

God has always been big on one generation teaching and guiding the next (See Deut. 6:6-7; Eph. 6:4). This idea is celebrated in Psalms: "We will not hide them from their children, but tell to the coming generation the glorious deeds of the Lord, and his might, and the wonders that he has done. He established a testimony...which he commanded our fathers to teach to their children" (Psa. 78:4-5).

Supporting the spread of the gospel to foreign lands is critical. Supporting the spread of the faith to children and grandchildren is no less so.

22

Daily Bible Reading: Ezekiel 27-28; 2 Timothy 2

Not About Satan

Devotional Text: Ezekiel 28:11-19

Paul encourages Timothy to be an "approved" and "unashamed" worker before God (2 Tim. 2:15). This is accomplished by "rightly handling the word of truth."

In Ezekiel 28 there is a text frequently mishandled. Chapter 28:11-19 is often cited as a text presenting the "fall of Satan" and even the rise of the supposed Anti-Christ.

The primary problem with this view is that there is nothing from this text that leads to such a conclusion. Instead, these ideas are drawn from other sources--many of them from the imaginations of men-- and as the wording of this text seems to support those ideas they are appropriated as "evidence" for the validity of the views.

The fact is, this text is very explicit that it's specifically about the king of Tyre. It's part of a larger prophecy beginning in chapter 26 which speaks of the city's great wealth, prominence, and power which undoubtedly led to the king's great pride. "Your heart is proud and you have said, 'I am a god'" (28:2).

God does not take kindly to such foolish notions, and thus prophesies the spectacular fall of this vain and arrogant king.

Rightly handling the "word of truth" sometimes forces us to abandon popular interpretations.

23

Daily Bible Reading: Ezekiel 29-31; 2 Timothy 3

Not Easy

Devotional Text: 2 Timothy 3:1

Simple does not mean easy. It can, but it doesn't always. Weight loss is simple-eat smarter and exercise more. But it sure isn't easy.

It's true with Scripture as well. Some very easily understood passages pose for us the greatest challenges.

For instance, the description of "times of difficulty" (2 Tim. 3:1ff): "people will be lovers of self, lovers of money, proud, arrogant, abusive, disobedient to their parents, ungrateful, unholy, heartless, unappeasable, slanderous, without selfcontrol," etc.

Is that not a spot-on description of our times? Alarming!

And what does Paul say a Christian should do in light of such difficult times? "Avoid such people" (v. 5).

At the very least, if we have any intentions of being a follower of Christ, we must exercise extreme care in the associations of our lives. Not that we become completely isolated and insulated. Jesus does not want us to be "out" of this world (see John 17:15). Salt and light must have a presence to have an effect (Matt. 5:13-14). But neither can we be casual about the spiritual impact swirling around us in the form of the people we encounter every day that we live.

These times, according to Paul, do qualify as "difficult." We need to know how to respond.

24
Daily Bible Reading: Ezekiel 32-33; 2 Timothy 4

How We Think About Death

Devotional Text: Ezekiel 33:11

Not to be a "Debbie-downer," but what do you think about death?

True, that is a pretty broad question, isn't it? Are we talking just death in general, or when someone in particular dies?

It's pretty obvious that generally speaking we try not to think about death at all if we can help it. And it's not anyone's death in particular, but rather what do we think when an evil person dies and when a good person dies?

Safe to say we are not too sad, and maybe even happy, when an evil person dies. At the very least there may be a sense of some satisfaction.

Now, when a good person dies, we are likely quite sad, especially if that death is "untimely."

Here's something to think about: God thinks just the opposite.

"As I live, declares the Lord God, I have no pleasure in the death of the wicked, but that the wicked turn from his way and live" (Ezek. 33:11).

"Precious in the sight of the Lord is the death of His saints" (Ps. 116:15).

Maybe we need to think again about how we think about death.

25

Daily Bible Reading: Psalms 130-134; Proverbs 28:10-28

Godly Fear

Devotional Text: Psalm 130:3-4

Surely we cannot question the importance of fearing God.

After all, it is the "beginning of wisdom" and the "whole duty of man" (Prov. 9:10; Eccl. 12:13).

At the same time, "It is a fearful thing to fall into the hands of the living God" (Heb. 10:31). It seems nearly contradictory, doesn't it? Be afraid of God and yet be drawn to Him because of His great love and mercy?

Maybe this Psalm will help: "If you, O Lord should mark iniquities, O Lord, who could stand? But with you there is forgiveness, that you may be feared" (Psa. 130:3-4).

It is a terrifying thing to consider how our sins condemn us before our Holy God. But it is also He that forgives. That reality leads us to "fear" Him. We are in awe of Him; holy and pure. He is willing--through no virtue of our own-to forgive and so save us from the condemnation that is rightfully ours.

The thoughtful and considered response to this reality is godly fear.

26

Daily Bible Reading: Ezekiel 34-36; 1 Peter 1:1-12

Faith's Results

Devotional Text: 1 Peter 1:7

Do you pursue a "results-based" faith?

A quick "Google" search of the internet gives first-page results showing this descriptive phrase applied in many ways: results-based management, accountability, training, planning, evaluation, and leadership.

A reading of 1 Peter 1:7 shows the concept as applied to faith. Peter is concerned that our faith produces the desired results, that is "praise and glory and honor at the revelation of Jesus Christ."

That makes sense.

But here's something that may not, at least on the surface. Peter said it is the "tested genuineness" of our faith that leads to the desired results. What does he mean by that?

He's talking about the "various trials" the child of God must endure that have the effect of purifying our faith (v. 6). It's just like gold being purified, or "tested," by fire as impurities are burned out, leaving the genuine article.

So, if we want the desired results, it requires the testing process.

Back to our original question: Do you pursue a "results-based" faith?

27

Daily Bible Reading: Ezekiel 37-38; 1 Peter 1:13-2:12

Beyond Ludicrous

Devotional Text: Ezekiel : 37:1-3

I don't like my steaks rare. I've heard the jokes about people who like their steaks so rare that "a skilled veterinarian could heal that."

That's funny, or at least it's intended to be, because it's beyond ludicrous.

Such also is the case, except for the funny part, when God asked Ezekiel whether or not dry bones could live (Ezekiel 37:1-3). That's just crazy.

Ezekiel, though, spoke judiciously: "O Lord God, you know."

Sure enough, God caused those bones to reform into skeletons; ligaments, muscle and tendons and muscle appeared, and finally skin covered them. Finally Ezekiel prophesied and "the breath came into them, and they lived" (Ezek. 37:7-10).

We ought not be too quick to pronounce what can or cannot be. Whether it's a marriage all but over, a Christian life far astray, a relationship long left for dead, a congregation lost under a mass of tradition and indifference, a nation falling further into unrighteousness, or whatever. The simple fact is, what appears impossible to us is not for God.

Is it all over? Is all hope gone? Is there even a whisper of a chance? The Lord knows.

28

Daily Bible Reading: Ezekiel 39-40; 1 Peter 2:13-3:7

Jesus' Steps

Devotional Text: 1 Peter 2:21

We talk about following in Jesus' steps. And we should; it's biblical. That very wording is used in 1 Peter 2:21. The idea is also found elsewhere (1 Pet 4:1; 1 John 2:6).

Years ago Charles Sheldon wrote an impactful book using Peter's words. It was titled *In His Steps*. That book prompted an earlier version of the more recent WWJD phenomenon. Following Jesus was taken very seriously.

Or was it?

Peter's point is that we should be willing, like Jesus, to endure ill-treatment. He was sinless yet He was reviled, but He did not respond in kind. "When He suffered, He did not threaten" (1 Peter 2:21-23).

What prompted this discussion? "If when you do good and suffer for it you endure, this is a gracious thing in the sight of God" (1 Peter. 2:20). So whether or not we are following in Jesus' steps--or doing what Jesus would do--is determined when we suffer as a result of the good we've done.

So what is it? Cry foul? Complain? Retaliate? Throw up our hands and quit?

Or endure?

The right path is unmistakable. It's marked by Jesus' steps when He went before us.

29

Daily Bible Reading: Ezekiel 41-43; 1 Peter 3:8-4:11

The Value of Negative Emotion

Devotional Text: Ezekiel 43:10

Human emotions are at the same time wonderful and horrible. There's nothing so grand as overflowing joy and indescribable love; and nothing so painful as grief or tortuous regret. Naturally, we are drawn to the sweet and repulsed by the bitter.

We are mistaken when we think that life is necessarily better when we can maximize the former and eliminate the latter. Modern child rearing seems to have bought in to this philosophy—no negative response ever to any child.

God doesn't think that way. He knows the value of and incorporated negative emotions as He dealt with His own people. Ezekiel's prophecy about the now-in-ruins-for-fourteen-years temple was intended to induce shame among the Israelites now in exile (43:10).

God was not being mean or capricious. But He wanted it impressed permanently on the conscience of this people that their unfaithfulness to Him had brought about this deplorable circumstance. The beautiful temple and all it represented was destroyed and in ruins. Their own actions deprived them of the glories of God's blessing.

Robbing our lives and the lives of others of negative emotions can have terrible consequences. We need the negative to move us to the positive.

30
Daily Bible Reading: Ezekiel 44-45; 1 Peter 4:12-5:14

Being a Christian

Devotional Text: 1 Peter 4:16

Here's an interesting little exercise. To the amazement of most people, the word "Christian" only appears a grand total of three times in the New Testament; that's right, only three. One of those is here in 1 Peter 4:16 (the other two are Acts 11:26 and 26:28).

If we are to be concerned with using Bible words in Bible ways--and I believe we really should be--then notice how the word is used by Peter.

In reading verses 15-17 there are some synonymous words and phrases used that tie to "Christian." For instance, "the household of God" (v. 17) is a reference to the same individuals as is the pronoun "us". Then, at the end of that same verse, a contrast is made between those whom Peter calls "Christians" and "those who do not obey the gospel of God."

Though we cannot pursue these ideas in this brief piece, looking further at God's household (1 Pet. 2:5; 1 Tim. 3:15; Eph. 2:19; Heb. 3:6; 10:21) and obedience to the gospel (1 Pet. 1:22; John 3:36; Heb. 5:9) will help clarify our thinking as to the biblical concept of being a Christian.

We can either allow our faith to be shaped and molded by Scripture or by popular ideas and usage. I know which I prefer.

DECEMBER

1

Daily Bible Reading: Ezekiel 46-48; 2 Peter 1

A Little Assurance is a Good Thing

Devotional Text: Ezekiel 48:35

We all need assurance. We need to know some things are true and real. The reason being that sometimes life seems to argue to the contrary.

So, in Revelation for instance, John writes to Christians beginning to feel the pressure and even persecution of the mighty Roman Empire. God has allowed John to see into heaven and sure enough, God is on His throne and in control. How reassuring.

The very end of Ezekiel is not unlike that. Remember, God's people were off in Babylonian captivity, their beloved Jerusalem lay in ruins, and God's own house had been destroyed. They needed assurance, and now.

The last vision, among many in the book, is of a city that God's people will occupy. The very last bit of information provided and also the very last words of this book are the city's name: "The Lord is there" (Ezek. 48:35).

No matter what happens, how bleak life may become, how isolated we may feel, or how hopeless our circumstance may appear, remember, the Lord is there.

Or in Jesus' own words, the very last of Matthew's book, "I am with you always, to the end of the age" (Matt. 28:20).

2

Daily Bible Reading: Psalm 135-137; Proverbs 29:1-27

Fully Alive

Devotional Text: Proverbs 29:11

Let's get philosophical for a moment. When is a person fully human? When are we fully alive? I don't mean in the sense of when life and personhood begins; that's another discussion. Rather, when are we actually what God created us to be as human beings?

Let's approach it this way: it is argued that this happens when we give full expression to ourselves, whenever we pursue and express whatever we think or feel or desire. Then, it is said, we are fully alive and fully human. That might seem to be so, but it's not what God--the one who made us in the first place--says.

"A fool gives full vent to his spirit, but a wise man quietly holds it back" (Prov. 29:11).

When the apostle Paul discussed faith in Christ with a Roman ruler, Felix, he spoke about self-control among other things (Acts 24:25). Further, when our lives are guided by God's Spirit as opposed to simply following the desire of the flesh, selfcontrol is one of the results (Gal. 5:23).

And don't forget that Jesus said the first requirement to following Him is to deny self. Thus, by losing our life we will actually find it (Matt. 10:38-39; 16:24).

We are, then, fully alive.

3
Daily Bible Reading: Daniel 1-2; 2 Peter 2

The Best Defense

Devotional Text: 2 Peter 2:1

I dislike being lied to. We all do. It's just wrong at the most fundamental level. God's righteousness is nowhere more simply yet profoundly expressed than when the Bible says it is impossible for Him to lie (Heb. 6:18).

This is why it is so disturbing when we are told that there will be false teachers (2 Pet. 2:1). They will act "secretly" and "exploit" their victims. The fruit of their efforts is "destruction" (vv. 1-3).

How in the world does one protect himself from such an insidious threat?

Notice these three references in this same chapter, all different but speaking of the same thing: "the way of truth," "the right way," and "the way of righteousness" (vv. 2, 15, 21).

Each of them speaks to a wrong behavior in respect to this "way"-- to blaspheme, forsake, and turn back.

So, how do we keep from falling victim to these liars? It's to know and embrace and love and follow the way that is true and right and righteous.

In this instance, the best defense is a good offense.

4

Daily Bible Reading: Daniel 3-4; 2 Peter 3

What's My Limit?

Devotional Text: Daniel 3:17-18

This thought is a little heavy. It's not a warm, fuzzy, feel-good kind of thought. But sometimes we need to venture out of the shallow end of the pool into some deeper waters.

What is the limit of your serving God? I mean, at what point would you say, "I can go no further with God"? Not every believer draws that line at the same place.

Think about the words of the three Israelite boys who refused to bow down to Nebuchadnezzar's image, even though the king explicitly commanded it be done and threatened to burn them alive if they didn't. They believed "our God whom we serve is able to deliver us." They then added, "But if not...we will not serve your gods" (Dan. 3:17-18).

The limit of their serving God extended beyond their own lives. They would willingly die rather than to deny God.

They were like Job, who said, "Though He slay me, I will hope in Him" (Job 13:15).

God, and my service to Him, exceeds the value of my life, as precious as it may be to me.

Where have I drawn my line?

5

Daily Bible Reading: Daniel 5-6; Jude

Jesus Did That?

Devotional Text: Jude 5

Unless you were reading from the English Standard Version, you wouldn't have noticed this. It's in verse 5 of Jude. "Now I want to remind you, although you once fully knew it, that Jesus, who saved a people out of the land of Egypt, afterward destroyed those who did not believe."

Jesus is identified as the one who saved the Israelites from the Egyptians. Most other translations say "Lord." Without getting into the questions regarding manuscript evidence for the different readings, I want to point out the fact of Jesus' activity prior to His arrival as Mary's baby in Bethlehem. Remember that 1 Corinthians 10:4 speaks of Jesus' sustaining presence with the people of Israel as they wandered in the wilderness. Most notable is His engagement in the creation process (see Heb. 1:2 and John 1:3, for instance).

Of course the vast majority of our information about Jesus' activity focuses on His coming to earth to fulfill God's purpose for humanity's salvation by His sacrifice for our sin. But knowing of His involvement with God from the very beginning in all that God was doing only enhances our wonder and awe for our marvelous Savior!

6
Daily Bible Reading: Daniel 7-8; Revelation 1

Knowing God Better

Devotional Text: Daniel 7:9,18

Here's an interesting approach to Bible study. After studying a text to learn its primary meaning and message, which should always be the chief aim, ask the question, "What does this text teach me about...?" You can end that sentence however you wish: God, Jesus, the Holy Spirit, salvation, the church, Christian living, etc.

Something intriguing happens when this exercise is pursued in Daniel 7 regarding God. There we find two interesting designations for God. One is "Ancient of Days" (vv. 9, 13, 22) and the other is "Highest One" (vv. 18, 22, 25, 27). Not only do these "names" highlight particular features of the Almighty, they are unique to Daniel 7, being found nowhere else in Scripture.

As we pursue an ever-growing and deepening knowledge of God, we are indebted to Daniel for these unique insights.

7

Daily Bible Reading: Daniel 9-11; Revelation 2

He Knows

Devotional Text: Revelation 2:2

When Jesus says, "I know," how does that make me feel?

One of the frequently repeated refrains of the letters to the seven churches of Asia Minor is the fact that Jesus knows. Eight times in these letters He says, "I know," and five times in chapter 2 (vv. 2, 3, 9, 13, 19).

I should feel assurance that Jesus knows. He knows my heart, He knows my deeds, He knows my sorrows, He knows my pains and my hurts. I am strengthened by the fact that He is caring and compassionate, that He is kind and loving, and that He possesses the power and authority to make a difference.

I should feel ashamed that Jesus knows. Yes, He knows my weaknesses and my failings, He knows my unkind and unholy thoughts, He knows my pettiness and selfishness. I cannot hide my "warts" and inadequacies from Him like I mask them from others. He knows, and I am ashamed.

Because He knows I should be motivated to action. I should be asking for help and forgiveness. I should be pursuing His solutions for my failings. I should be drawing closer to the one who knows me so well, knowing He's drawing closer to me (Jas. 4:8).

You see, we also know. We know that He is ready and willing to forgive. We know that He is able to heal and to help. We know that He wants to bless, not condemn. What a joy to know that not only does He know, but we know.

8

Daily Bible Reading: Daniel 12; Hosea 1-3; Revelation 3

Why Does He Love?

Devotional Text: Hosea 1:1-9

"How would you feel?"

That question has become a mantra for my wife. One of her greatest concerns in life is for people to be treated well. She believes we should always think about how we are treating others and ask how it would feel to be treated the same way.

Taking nothing away from her, I think Jesus taught the same thing. We call it "the golden rule" (Matt. 7:12).

That's exactly what God was getting at with Hosea. That is to try to show them how He felt because of the way they had treated Him. That's why He commanded Hosea to marry a prostitute, settle down and have children. Then, when she ran off and did the prostitute thing again, go take her back (Hos. 1:1-9; 3:1-5).

It's chilling to know that God thinks of the relationship with His people this way. It was true of Israel and it's true of the church today.

But even more remarkable than all of that is the fact of God's unfathomable love. Why, oh why, does He love us so?

9

Daily Bible Reading: Psalms 138-141; Proverbs 30:1-17

God is There

Devotional Text: Psalm 139:1-12

People baffle me.

As a preacher I often hear comments about changed behavior in the presence of the preacher. Yes, it's sometimes in jest, but sometimes not.

"You better straighten up, the preacher's here." Or, "If I'd known I was going to see you today [the preacher], I would have dressed a little differently." Or maybe it's an apology for some choice language in my presence.

You don't answer to the preacher.

But you do answer to God.

So, think about the words of Psalm 139:1-12. Two points are eloquently made. First, God knows you better than you know yourself, including your thoughts and intentions. There is nothing about "you" that is hidden from Him.

Second, there is no place you can go to hide from God. Nowhere.

So it's not the presence of the preacher, or an elder, or your mother or your spouse that should be the motivation for right behavior, it's the presence of God--and He's always there.

10
Daily Bible Reading: Hosea 4-7; Revelation 4

Why Worship God?

Devotional Text: Revelation 4:8,11

Why do you worship God? I mean, what is it about God that motivates you to give Him worship?

Or have you ever thought about it? Have you just done it because you were told to, were taught to, or saw others do it? Have you thought about it any further than that it's because He is the broad and all-encompassing "great" or "awesome"?

Through John, God gives us a privileged view into His very throne room in heaven (Rev. 4). There, around God's throne, are four incredible creatures and the 24 elders. Both groups are continuously worshipping God. The creatures do so because of God's holiness and eternal nature (v. 8). The elders worship God because He is the creator (v. 11).

Those aren't the only reasons God is worthy of worship, but they are specific ones.

So, again, why do you worship God? Instead of the usual broad and unspecified approach, why not praise Him quite specifically for one of the endless reasons He deserves our worship?

11
Daily Bible Reading: Hosea 8-11; Revelation 5

Harvest Law

Devotional Text: Hosea 10:12

I have lived in farm country--rice, cotton, soybeans, and corn mostly. That didn't make me a farmer, but I lived among abundant evidence of the validity of the law of the harvest; you harvest what you sow and more of it.

This law doesn't apply just to farming; it's a spiritual law too. "Do not be deceived: God is not mocked, for whatever one sows, that will he also reap" (Gal. 6:9; see also 2 Cor. 9:6).

One way of looking at this is to think about what you are reaping now. Is it what you wanted? Are you pleased with the present "harvest" of your life? If not, it's time to change the seed that you're sowing.

That was Hosea's message. The people were getting a lousy "harvest," and it was no mystery why; "You have plowed iniquity; you have reaped injustice; you have eaten the fruit of lies," (Hos. 10:13). Or, "For they sow the wind, and they shall reap the whirlwind" (v. 7).

The solution is no mystery either; "Sow for yourselves righteousness; reap steadfast love; break up your fallow ground, for it is the time to seek the Lord, that he may come and rain righteousness upon you" (Hos. 10:12).

We presently reap what we have formerly sown. As Paul warned, don't be deceived about that.

12

Daily Bible Reading: Hosea 12-14; Joel 1; Revelation 6

Not Like We Are

Devotional Text: Revelation 6:10

The thing about God that troubles us the most is that He is not just like we are. He doesn't think like we do or do what we would do. And thank goodness for that.

But think about it. Why is it that we think, and even say, things like, "Why doesn't God...?" or "How come God...?" or any number of statements like this? Is it not because God isn't doing or hasn't done like we would do? And that troubles us. We need to get comfortable with it, though, because this is who God is.

Even in heaven itself, according to John's revelation, the souls of martyred saints in heaven are asking, "How long before you will judge and avenge our blood?" (Rev. 6:10).

God hadn't addressed their unjust deaths in as timely a manner as they would have liked.

No, God is not like we are, does not think like we think, and does not act as we would act. If He did, He would be exactly like us. How horrible that would be.

We need a God who is bigger, who knows more, is wiser, can see the future as clearly as the past, who is infinite in power and mercy and compassion and...well, who is everything we are not.

I'd rather have a God like that and live with the discomfort of His not being just like me.

13

Daily Bible Reading: Joel 2-3; Revelation 7

The Day of the Lord

Devotional Text: Joel 3:14

It's interesting to read the prophet Joel on this date, December 13, for two reasons. One is that back in 2012, one week after that day, December 20--to hear some people tell it--it was to be the earth's last day, as December 21 would usher in a cataclysmic end of the world. (Remember the Myan calendar hubbub?)

The second reason is that Joel keeps talking about the coming "day of the Lord" (1:15; 2:1, 2, 11, 31; 3:14). "Alas for the day! For the day of the Lord is near, and as destruction from the Almighty it comes...a great and very awesome day."

But Joel isn't talking about the end of the world and certainly not December 21, 2012, but rather God's coming judgment against Judah and Jerusalem. Because it is coming He warns his people to repent (2:12-13). And what happens as a result of that day, whether for good or bad, all depends on the decision His people make in response.

"Multitudes, multitudes, in the valley of decision! For the day of the Lord is near in the valley of decision" (3:14).

The Bible speaks as well about another coming day in which God will judge the world (Acts 17:31). It too is a day for which we must prepare and do so by decisions we now make in regard to the one who will be our judge--Jesus Christ.

We have our own valley of decision in light of this yet-to-come "day of the Lord."

368

14
Daily Bible Reading: Amos 1-4; Revelation 8

Jesus Knows

Devotional Text: Revelation 8:1

Revelation 8 finds us in the middle of the pageantry of events unleashed by the successive opening of seven seals on the scroll from God's right hand.

John watches these events as played out from the throne room of God. The pageant is immense and grand and terrible. Theologians and Bible expositors wrestle for meaning.

This is challenging to be sure, but not impossible as a blessing is assigned to those who "hear and who keep" what it says (Rev. 1:3).

What is certain, and most reassuring, is the fact that the only one able to unlock the seals, who knows and understands all that is to transpire, the only one found in a search of heaven worthy to take the sealed scroll from God's right hand was the Lamb (Rev. 5:16).

This Lamb, of course, is Jesus, the "lion of the tribe of Judah" and the "Root of David."

The same Jesus who unveils these incredible happenings is the one who knows and cares and guards my own little life.

15

Daily Bible Reading: Amos 5-7; Revelation 9

Genuine Religion

Devotional Text: Amos 5:6,14

"Seek the Lord and live...seek good and not evil" (Amos 5:6, 14).

Could it really be that simple? Could a people who are God's fall so far that the answer to their dilemma is as fundamental as to seek God and seek good?

Apparently so.

Why had it not become apparent to them sooner. Why did it require a message from God's prophet?

Maybe because all the while they had remained a religious people. Their religion masked their own spiritual depravity.

Worship had continued. Their assemblies, offerings, and songs never ceased. But God hated them all (Amos 5:21-23). He despised and rejected them. He would not look; He would not listen.

The remedy? What was seeking God and seeking good supposed to look like?

"But let justice roll down like waters, and righteousness like an everflowing stream"(Amos 5:24).

The expression of genuine religion isn't found in worship assemblies, but in lives lived with righteousness and justice. Lives, then, that are like God can give worship that He honors, not hates.

16
Daily Bible Reading: Psalm 142-144; Proverbs 30:18-35

Big or Small

Devotional Text: Proverbs 30:24-28

We like big; big games, big paychecks, big corporations, big trucks, big celebrities, and big orders of fries. Not everyone does and not all the time, but obviously, big sells.

When seeking wisdom, Proverbs says, go small!

Consider these things that though small are "exceedingly wise": the ant, the rock badger, the locust and the lizard (Prov. 30:24-28). Wisdom is not restricted by size.

None of these four possess strength (ants), might (rock badger), a great leader (locusts), or overpowering presence (lizard). None of that would make them admirable or worthy of emulation. Their wisdom does.

They may not be big in some ways, but they are in others.

One of the "truths" of coaching legend John Wooden was to not allow what you don't have to get in the way of what you do have. Not everyone has what it takes to be big, but we can--even the smallest of us--be wise.

17
Daily Bible Reading: Amos 8-9; Obadiah; Revelation 10

Hungry?

Devotional Text: Revelation 10:9

Eat it.

Those are the simple instructions given to John by the voice speaking from heaven. They are reminiscent cf words given to both Jeremiah and Ezekiel (15:16ff; 3:8-3:3).

The heavenly voice promised sweetness in the mouth and bitterness in the stomach (Rev 10:9).

We understand the sweetness of God's word. It is encouragement and help and instruction and life. It provides guidance and instruction, comfort and hope, and light and joy. That is all sweet to the taste.

But, bitterness? What about when God tells us what we don't want to hear? To give over ourselves in complete submission? To love our enemies? To forgive?

Or when He rebukes, reproves or corrects? Calls us to repent or pronounces judgment?

Whether that word is to us bitter or sweet very much depends on our disposition and outlook. The truth is, God's word will always accomplish its purpose and never return to Him empty (Isa. 55:11).

So go ahead; eat it.

18

Daily Bible Reading: Jonah 1-4; Micah 1; Revelation 11

A Bigger Issue

Devotional Text: Jonah 4:1

There's more to Jonah than a fish story.

Incredible as that is, the bigger issue--yes, even bigger than the fishsurfaces afterward. The whole fish scenario served to motivate Jonah to do God's will.

That's a big issue. Jonah's adventure of running from God and winding up in the belly of this great fish drives this point home effectively.

But now for lesson two. Jonah became upset when the people of Nineveh repented at this preaching and God did not bring His threatened punishment. By use of a vine and a worm (Jonah 4) God showed the prophet that though he had done God's will by delivering His message to Nineveh, he did not share God's compassion and mercy.

It is one thing, and a desirable thing, to do God's will. It is entirely another thingand an even more important oneto share God's character.

19

Daily Bible Reading: Micah 2-5; Revelation 12

Know the Enemy

Devotional Text: Revelation 12:3,9

Many things about Revelation are challenging at best and mostly downright confounding.

Other things are crystal clear.

Satan, for instance, is the sworn enemy of God, His people, and His cause. As the second half of the book opens here in chapter 12, Satan is identified as a "great red dragon" (compare 12:3 and 9).

His opposition to God and all that He is doing is evident as the dragon tries to eat the male child as the woman is giving birth (12:1-2,4). God rescues the child and the woman escapes, being cared for and protected by God (vv. 5-6, 13-16).

Next the dragon does battle with the angel Michael. Satan is defeated as the advancement of God's cause is announced (12:7-12).

Furious at his defeat, Satan makes war on the rest of the woman's offspring, "on those who keep the commandments of God and hold to the testimony of Jesus" (v. 17). Now who does that sound like?

It's quite clear that Satan is God's enemy and if I'm on God's side, he's my enemy.

In the words of a Bible class song from childhood, "One, two, three, the devil's after me..."

20

Daily Bible Reading: Micah 6-7; Nahum 1; Revelation 13

Beginning With Me

Devotional Text: Micah 6:7-8

If some is good, more is better. Right?

It is correct that God desires worship. Jesus said God is seeking true worshippers to worship Him (John 4:23). The Bible encourages and promotes offering worship to God (Heb. 12:28).

So, whatever it is that we're giving to God in worship, let's give more, and what's more, let's give what is of the highest possible worth. Does that not sound like a formula for pleasing our Creator?

Apparently not.

> *Will the Lord be pleased with thousands of rams, with ten thousands of rivers of oil? Shall I give my firstborn for my transgression, the fruit of my body for the sin of my soul? He has told you, O man, what is good; and what does the Lord require of you but to do justice, and to love kindness, and to walk humbly with your God* (Micah 6:7-8).

Improving worship, that is, God's acceptance of it and of me-doesn't begin with worship at all. It begins with me.

21

Daily Bible Reading: Nahum 2-3, Habakkuk 1, Revelation 14

Not Just Today, But Every Day

Devotional Text: Revelation 14:6-7

This date a few years ago captured the world's attention and imagination. It really was a world-wide phenomenon with countless people convinced it was the world's last day. Too bad.

Not because people are interested in this kind of thing, but because it distracts from the truth about it all. And the truth--from God, not an ancient Central American Indian civilization--is that the end is indeed coming, there's just no calendar for it (Matt. 24:36, 42, 44).

The most important feature of that day is not the catastrophic destruction of the world (see 2 Pet. 3:10), but rather the return of Jesus and the judgment of all mankind (Matt. 25:31-46).

John's vision of Revelation 14 speaks to that day when the hour of God's judgment has come (Rev. 14:6-7). Two quite notable things are revealed here. One, preparation is made for it by the proclamation of the eternal gospel to "those who dwell on earth, to every nation and tribe and language and people." Does that not put us in mind of the "Great Commission" (Matt. 28:19-20; Mark 16:15-16)?

Second, it demands of man that he "[f]ear God and give Him glory... and worship Him."

So, as that date came and went, may we be reminded of what should be happening today--and every day--in view of the real end that is coming.

22

Daily Bible Reading: Habakkuk 2-3; Zephaniah 1; Revelation 15

Keep Silent

Devotional Text: Habakkuk 2:20

Movement means life.

Dr. Frankenstein strained to see movement in the monster's limbs to confirm it was alive.

Rookie parents anxiously look to see their newborn's little chest rise and fall as she sleeps, just to make sure she's still breathing.

A quiet little town is deemed "dead" by an antsy teen just because there is so little activity.

Movement means life.

Or not.

It can mean spiritual death, or at least weakness.

True, God's children are to be "always abounding in the work of the Lord" (1 Cor. 15:58).

But so too are we to "keep silence before Him" (Hab. 2:20) and "be still and know that I am God" (Ps. 46:10).

It's not always about being busy. It's not even always about voicing praise to God. Sometimes it's about being silent and still in His presence. If we are unable to do so, it may speak loudly to our spiritual weakness.

23

Daily Bible Reading: Psalm 145-147; Proverbs 31:1-9

The Glory of God Through Time

Devotional Text: Psalm 145:3

God is eternal, as are His might and power and compassion and love and knowledge and...well, we get the picture. "Great is the Lord, and greatly to be praised, and his greatness is unsearchable" (Ps. 145:3).

Therefore, His glory spans all of time, that is, it too is eternal.

"I will extol you, my God and my King, and bless your name forever and ever...and praise your name forever and ever" (Ps. 145:12).

We, on the other hand, are not "forever." God's days are without number, unlike our own. Still, from man's limited perspective God's glory continues and we participate in extending that glory beyond the number of our days.

"One generation shall commend your works to another, and shall declare your mighty acts" (Ps. 145:4).

So we have the eternal span of time (?) and we have the generational span of time. But one more span of time remains: today.

"Every day I will bless you and praise your name..." (Ps. 145:2).

The glory of God spanning through all of time is reason for me to give Him glory today and every day.

24
Daily Bible Reading: Zephaniah 2-3; Haggai 1; Revelation 16

Thwarting God's Will

Devotional Text: Revelation 16:9,11

Are you more powerful than God?

Well, of course not. That's ridiculous.

But what is not ridiculous is that God will not violate one's free will. That is, He allows us to make choices that result in outcomes that He does not want or intend.

For instance, in Revelation 16, twice it is stated that as a result of bowls of wrath of God being poured out, men blasphemed the name of God and did not repent (vv. 9,11).

Repentance of sinful men is what God wants. Jesus came preaching, "Repent for the kingdom of heaven is at hand" (Matt. 4:17). Peter's first gospel sermon called for men to "repent and be baptized" (Acts 2:38).

God wanted men to be motivated to repent, instead they blasphemed Him; not the outcome He wanted. So respectful, though, is God to human free will--his freedom to choose--that He allows those choices to be made.

More powerful than God? No, but in possession of a power that God, at least for now, will allow to trump His own purpose and desire.

Be careful!

25

Daily Bible Reading: Haggai 2; Zechariah 1-2; Revelation 17

Return to God

Devotional Text: Zechariah 1:3

That of which God is capable is beyond imagination. Paul, quoting Isaiah, said that not only have human eyes not seen nor ears heard, the heart of man can't even imagine what God has done on man's behalf (I Cor. 2:9).

That does not mean, though, that God is going to do everything that He could do. He has determined that sometimes what He does is going to depend on us.

Think about that for a moment.

God is waiting for me to act, so He can do the marvelous things He is quite capable of doing.

"Return to me, says the Lord of hosts, and I will return to you, says the Lord of hosts" (Zech. 1:3).

That sounds very much like James 4:8, "Draw near to God and He will draw near to you."

We cannot even begin to imagine all that is entailed in God's returning and drawing near and being with us.

But I do want to find out.

26

Daily Bible Reading: Zechariah 3-6; Revelation 18

Eternal or Economic Security?

Devotional Text: Revelation 18:2

The Bible is timeless, for one reason, because people are people. The Bible addresses those issues and concerns that are fundamental to humanity, no matter where or when one might live.

In Revelation 18 an angel from heaven announces the monumental fall of "Babylon" (Rev. 18:2). A reference, I believe, to the nation of Rome --the powerful and decadent enemy and persecutor of God's people.

Notice two reactions to this announcement: saints and apostles and prophets rejoice (v. 20) while merchants weep and mourn (v. 11).

Why? Rejoicing is because her unrighteous ways and influence are ended and mourning because she had afforded opportunities for great wealth and income.

Telling isn't it? Think about it. What matters to us? The kingdom of God and His righteousness or the opportunity for personal gain and wealth? Eternal security or economic stability?

Undoubtedly "Babylon's" fall sent economic shockwaves through the ancient world. But was the world really better or worse for her absence?

Are my own greatest concerns for a strong fiscal standing or for "holiness without which no one will see the Lord" (Heb. 12:14)?

27

Daily Bible Reading: Zechariah 7-9; Revelation 19

Simple, Not Easy

Devotional Text: Zechariah 7:9-10

It's not a mystery and neither is it difficult.

Then why do people have so much trouble doing God's will? Seriously.

> *Thus says the LORD of hosts, 'Render true judgments, show kindness and mercy to one another, do not oppress the widow, the fatherless, the sojourner, or the poor, and let none of you devise evil against another in your heart'* (Zech. 7:9-10).

And it's not like this is the only time God has said this. "He has told you, O man, what is good; and what does the LORD require of you but to do justice, and to love kindness, and to walk humbly with your God?" (Micah 6:8).

Or how about Proverbs 3:3, "Do not let kindness and truth leave you; Bind them around your neck. Write them on the tablet of your heart" (NASB)?

You might also look at passages like Ezek. 18:5-9; Amos 5:24; Isa. 1:16-17; James 1:27.

The formula is simple: be good and kind and do what is right.

But simple, I suppose, does not necessarily mean easy.

28

Daily Bible Reading: Zechariah 10-13; Revelation 20

Most Unpleasant

Devotional Text: Revelation 20:10

That doesn't sound pleasant at all! "Lake of fire and brimstone," "tormented day and night forever and ever" (Rev. 20:10).

Unpleasant indeed.

Joining the devil, the beast, and the false prophet there, will be everyone whose name is not found written the book of life (v. 14).

This, of course, is a description of hell and the final judgment. In addition to the book of life, the dead will be judged "from the things that are written in the books, according to what they had done" (v. 12).

Remember Jesus' words? "Do not marvel at this, for an hour is coming when all who are in the tombs will hear his voice and come out, those who have done good to the resurrection of life, and those who have done evil to the resurrection of judgment" (John 5:28-29).

What you do-or don't do--matters.

It matters in judgment.

It matters eternally.

If there is any intention of avoiding hell's unpleasantness, then concern for what I do today is paramount.

29
Daily Bible Reading: Zechariah 14, Malachi 1-2; Revelation 21

The Last Word

Devotional Text: Malachi 1:2

It's a bit ironic. The prophet Malachi repeatedly uses a literary formula in his message. It is, "...says the Lord. But you say..." (see 1:2,6,7; 2:14; 3:7,8,13).

What's the irony? The formula is essentially a question of who will have the last word, the Lord or us? And, this is the book of Malachi, the last book of the Old Testament. God's last word (under the Old Covenant), as it were.

This really is a fundamental question of our existence; will we allow God to have the last word?

Or do we feel compelled to "explain away" His word? To rationalize our behavior that violates His will? Or to place our own finite intellect and knowledge above His omniscience?

Maybe that's what Malachi's peers are getting at: "Be silent before the Lord God!" "The Lord is in His holy temple; let all the earth keep silence before Him." (Zeph. 1:7; Hab. 2:20).

When "the Lord says," it is not time for us to speak, but to listen.

30
Daily Bible Reading: Psalm 148-150; Proverbs 31:10-31

She is Strong

Devotional Text: Proverbs 31:17,25

Twice in the famous "Worthy Woman" description of Proverbs 31, her wardrobe is discussed. On neither occasion is there mention of the clothing's label or her fashion sense or the price tag.

Instead, it says, "she dresses herself with strength" and "strength and dignity are her clothing" (vv. 17,25).

Interesting isn't it that another well-known statement regarding women, specifically wives, is Paul's "weaker vessel" reference of 1 Peter 3:7?

So which is it? Is she weak or is she strong?

The latter reference is not a description of the woman but rather the husband's attitude toward his wife. It is one of honor, treating her with care and gentility. The husband deals with his wife "as with someone weaker" (NASB), not that she is.

Far from it, the "excellent wife" who is "more precious than jewels" clothes herself with "strength and dignity" (Prov. 31:10,25). And a wise husband not only recognizes her strength but draws on it himself. Her strength is no threat to him as "she does him good, and not harm, all the days of her life" (v. 12).

A beautiful woman is a strong woman.

31
Daily Bible Reading: Malachi 3-4; Revelation 22

Final Words

Devotional Text: Revelation 22:21

Final words are important words.

The last words of a dying loved one are cherished. The final words of a departing, beloved leader endure. The closing words of a well-told story satisfy.

Final words are important words.

So it is with the Bible.

"The grace of the Lord Jesus be with all. Amen" (Rev. 22:21).

That's what it's all about--all of the Bible; all of the great events and characters; all of the power of God's miraculous works; all of the struggles and hardships; all of the history and law and poetry and prophecy and teaching and letters; all of the revelation and inspiration.

It's all about the grace of God found in the Lord Jesus and available to all.

Nothing more could we ever ask or want or receive.

May the Lord's grace be with you and with me.

INDEX

STRENGTH FOR THE JOURNEY:
A Daily Devotional Guide

David Deffenbaugh & Bill McFarland

ISBN # 978-0-9766703-5-3

Are you a daily Bible reader? If so, maximize your daily reading with Strength for the Journey. Designed to take you through the Bible in a year, plus provide you with insightful and uplifting devotionals from each day's Bible reading.

MORE STRENGTH FOR THE JOURNEY
A Daily Devotional Guide

Danny Boggs, Kirk Brothers, Bobby Dockery, & Neal Pollard

ISBN # 978-0-9766703-9-1

Designed to lead you in reading your Bible through in a year, this book provides a reading schedule along with insights and encouragements based on each day's reading text.

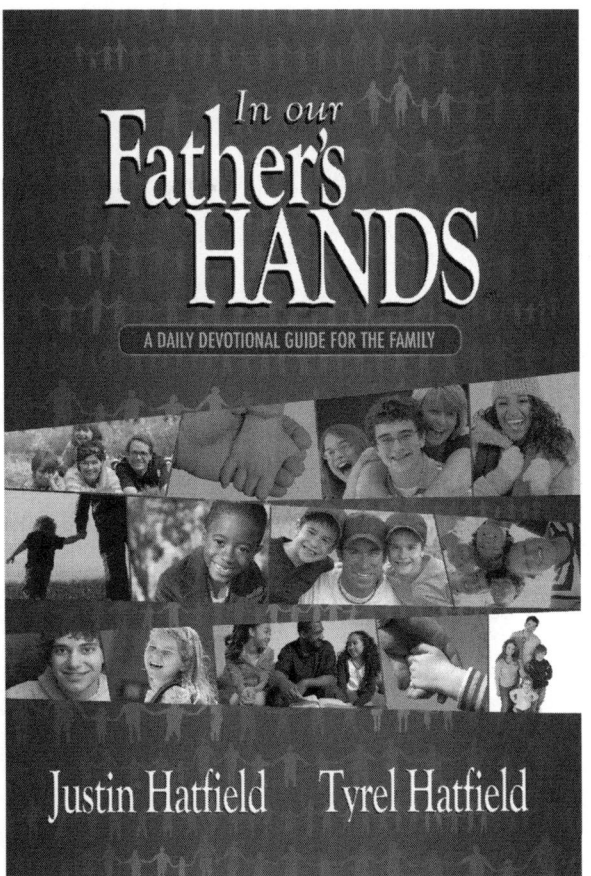

IN OUR FATHER'S HANDS:
A Daily Devotional Guide for the Family

Tyrel Hatfield & Justin Hatfield

ISBN # 978-0-9766703-4-6

Raising children who love and respect God's word is not an easy task. *In Our Father's Hands* will aid those parents who are dedicated to that purpose. Designed to take you through the Bible in a year, parents are provided with a devotional to share with their children each day.